The Art of Shadowplay

The Art of Shadowplay

Matthew Petchinsky

The Art of Shadowplay: Building Your Own Personal Myth
By: Matthew Petchinsky

Introduction

Understanding the Shadow: Embracing the Hidden Parts of Ourselves

Every human carries within them a shadow—a reservoir of unexamined desires, fears, and traits we often deny or suppress. This shadow is not an enemy but a mirror, reflecting aspects of ourselves that we hesitate to acknowledge. Carl Jung, the father of analytical psychology, emphasized that the shadow holds immense transformative power. To engage with it is to embark on a journey toward wholeness.

The shadow thrives in the unseen corners of our psyche, subtly influencing our decisions, relationships, and self-perception. It whispers through our moments of anger, envy, or fear, revealing truths we often ignore. Yet, rather than being a source of shame, the shadow is a wellspring of authenticity and creativity. By embracing these hidden parts of ourselves, we integrate the fragments of our identity, creating a harmonious balance between light and dark. This integration empowers us to live more fully, authentically, and with greater self-awareness.

This book begins by exploring this concept of the shadow, not as a foreboding force but as a treasure trove of self-discovery. You will learn to identify the shadow in your life, engage with it compassionately, and harness its energy to shape a life that reflects your truest self.

The Power of Myth: Shaping Reality Through Stories

Human beings are storytellers by nature. Since the dawn of time, myths have been our way of making sense of the world, our place in it, and the mysteries that lie beyond. From the epic tales of gods and heroes to the personal narratives we craft about our lives, stories are the lenses through which we view reality. Myths shape our beliefs, guide our choices, and define our identities.

At their core, myths are symbolic representations of universal truths. They provide us with archetypes—patterns of behavior and identity that resonate deeply within our subconscious. These archetypes, such as the Hero, the Lover, the Rebel, or the Sage, serve as mirrors of our inner selves and blueprints for our personal growth. By engaging with myth, we uncover a language for understanding our inner worlds and navigating the complexities of life.

This book delves into the transformative power of myth, not just as a cultural phenomenon but as a personal tool. You will explore how the myths you believe and the stories you tell yourself influence your perception of reality. By rewriting your personal myth, you gain the ability to reshape your life, aligning your actions and aspirations with your deepest truths.

How This Book Will Guide You to Craft Your Own Personal Myth

The journey to understanding and embracing your shadow, paired with the insights of myth, forms the foundation for building your own personal mythology. This book serves as a guide, offering practical tools and profound insights to help you weave a narrative that aligns with your authentic self.

Through the pages that follow, you will:

- **Explore the Shadow**: Learn techniques to identify and embrace the hidden aspects of your psyche, transforming fear and resistance into self-awareness and growth.
- **Decode Archetypes**: Understand the universal patterns of behavior and identity that influence your life, and discover how to integrate them into your personal narrative.
- **Craft Your Myth**: Engage in creative exercises and reflective practices to rewrite your story, allowing you to take control of your destiny and live a life of purpose.

This book is not a one-size-fits-all formula; it is a toolkit for self-discovery. Whether you seek to overcome obstacles, redefine your goals, or deepen your understanding of who you are, this journey will equip you with the clarity and courage to step into your power.

The pages ahead invite you to embrace the unknown, confront your fears, and step into the role of the storyteller of your own life. Are you ready to meet your shadow, rewrite your myth, and unlock the potential that lies within? The journey begins now.

Part 1: Foundations of Shadowplay

Chapter 1: What Is Shadowplay? The Art of Exploring the Unseen

Shadowplay is the delicate dance of light and dark within ourselves, a practice that invites us to explore the unseen corners of our psyche and embrace the mysteries that shape our identity. At its core, shadowplay is both an art and a science—a journey into the depths of the subconscious to uncover the hidden truths that influence our thoughts, actions, and emotions. This chapter provides a comprehensive understanding of shadowplay, its origins, its significance, and how it can transform your life.

Defining Shadowplay: A Path to Wholeness

The term "shadowplay" originates from the interplay of light and shadow that has long captivated artists, storytellers, and philosophers. In the context of self-exploration, shadowplay refers to the practice of engaging with the shadow self—the collection of traits, emotions, and desires that we repress or deny. These aspects often remain hidden from conscious awareness, yet they shape our behaviors and perceptions in profound ways.

Shadowplay is not about eliminating the shadow or overcoming it. Instead, it is about understanding and integrating these hidden aspects, allowing them to coexist with our conscious selves. This integration fosters a sense of wholeness, as we learn to embrace all parts of who we are, rather than just the aspects we deem acceptable.

The Origins of Shadowplay

The concept of the shadow has roots in many cultural and philosophical traditions. Carl Jung, a Swiss psychiatrist and psychoanalyst, was one of the first to formally introduce the idea in psychology. Jung described the shadow as the "dark side" of the personality, consisting of all the traits we reject and hide from the world. He believed that confronting the shadow was essential for personal growth, as it holds the potential for creativity, self-awareness, and transformation.

Beyond psychology, shadowplay finds resonance in mythology, spirituality, and art. Ancient myths often depict heroes venturing into the underworld to face their fears and emerge transformed—a metaphor for engaging with the shadow. In art, chiaroscuro (the dramatic use of light and dark) reflects the human fascination with contrasts and the interplay between visibility and obscurity.

Shadowplay builds on these traditions, combining introspection, creativity, and symbolic storytelling to navigate the complexities of the human psyche.

The Importance of Exploring the Unseen

Why should we explore the unseen aspects of ourselves? The answer lies in the profound impact of the shadow on our lives. The shadow often manifests in unconscious patterns—behaviors that seem out of character, emotional reactions that feel disproportionate, or recurring challenges that resist resolution. These patterns are clues, pointing to the unresolved aspects of the self.

By engaging in shadowplay, we gain:

1. **Self-Awareness**: Recognizing the shadow helps us understand the motivations and fears driving our actions, allowing us to make conscious choices.
2. **Emotional Freedom**: Repressed emotions lose their power when brought into the light, freeing us from guilt, shame, or fear.
3. **Authenticity**: Embracing the shadow enables us to live more authentically, as we accept ourselves fully—light and dark alike.
4. **Enhanced Relationships**: Understanding our own shadow fosters empathy for others, improving our relationships by reducing projection and judgment.

The Art of Shadowplay: Tools and Practices

Shadowplay is a deeply personal journey, but it is also a creative process that involves various tools and practices. These methods serve as guides, helping you navigate the often murky waters of the subconscious.

1. **Journaling**: Writing is a powerful tool for uncovering hidden thoughts and emotions. Reflective prompts can help you explore your fears, desires, and patterns of behavior.
2. **Dream Analysis**: Dreams often provide a window into the subconscious, revealing symbols and narratives that represent aspects of the shadow.
3. **Creative Expression**: Art, music, and storytelling allow you to engage with the shadow symbolically, giving form to the intangible.
4. **Meditation and Visualization**: Mindfulness practices create a safe space to observe your inner world, fostering insight and clarity.
5. **Mythic Archetypes**: Exploring archetypes—universal symbols found in myths and stories—can help you identify shadow aspects and understand their significance in your life.
6. **Therapeutic Practices**: Working with a therapist or guide trained in shadow work can provide valuable support and structure for your exploration.

The Challenges of Shadowplay

While shadowplay is transformative, it is not without its challenges. Confronting the shadow requires courage and honesty, as it often brings discomfort and resistance. The process may unearth painful memories, reveal uncomfortable truths, or challenge long-held beliefs. However, these challenges are a necessary part of the journey, as they pave the way for growth and healing.

Shadowplay as a Lifelong Practice

Shadowplay is not a one-time endeavor but a lifelong practice. The shadow evolves as we grow, presenting new opportunities for exploration and integration. By committing to this practice, we cultivate a deeper relationship with ourselves, one rooted in compassion, curiosity, and acceptance.

As you embark on the path of shadowplay, remember that the goal is not perfection but wholeness. Each step you take—no matter how small—is a victory in your journey toward self-discovery. In the chapters ahead, we will delve deeper into the tools, myths, and practices that will guide you in crafting your own personal myth, beginning with the foundational art of shadowplay. Let the exploration begin.

Chapter 2: The Role of Shadows in Mythology and Archetypes

Throughout history, myths have served as humanity's collective memory and spiritual compass, offering timeless insights into the human condition. Central to many myths is the concept of the shadow—a representation of our hidden fears, desires, and truths. In this chapter, we will explore how shadows manifest in mythology, their symbolic significance, and how archetypes illuminate our understanding of the human psyche. By understanding the role of shadows in myths and archetypes, we uncover profound tools for personal transformation and self-awareness.

Shadows in Mythology: Universal Symbols of the Unseen

Shadows have always been powerful symbols in mythology, representing the dualities inherent in existence: light and dark, known and unknown, good and evil. Across cultures, shadows are often depicted as manifestations of the human struggle with inner darkness, as well as guides to self-discovery and enlightenment.

1. **The Shadow as Adversary**

   In many myths, the shadow appears as a nemesis or antagonist. This figure embodies the traits the hero must confront to grow. Consider the myth of Theseus and the Minotaur. The labyrinth represents the subconscious, and the Minotaur—half-man, half-beast—is the shadow self, a terrifying amalgamation of the primal instincts we suppress. By defeating the Minotaur, Theseus conquers his inner fears and emerges transformed.

2. **The Shadow as Protector or Guide**

   Shadows can also take on protective or guiding roles. In Egyptian mythology, the shadow (known as the "Ka") was a vital part of the soul. It symbolized a person's essence and could guide them through the challenges of the afterlife. This dual nature of the shadow—as both feared and revered—reflects its complexity and its potential for aiding in self-awareness.

3. **The Descent into Darkness**

   Many myths feature a hero's descent into darkness, a symbolic journey into the shadow. In Greek mythology, Orpheus ventures into the Underworld to retrieve Eurydice, confronting the realm of the dead (a metaphor for the unconscious). Similarly, Inanna's descent into the Sumerian underworld symbolizes stripping away the ego to confront the shadow self and be reborn.

4. **Trickster Figures**

   Trickster archetypes, like Loki in Norse mythology or Coyote in Native American lore, represent shadow aspects of intelligence, cunning, and unpredictability. They challenge societal norms and force heroes to adapt, highlighting the role of chaos in growth.

Archetypes: The Building Blocks of the Psyche

Swiss psychiatrist Carl Jung developed the concept of archetypes—universal, symbolic patterns that reside in the collective unconscious. These archetypes appear in myths, dreams, and stories across cultures, offering a window into the shared human experience. Understanding archetypes provides a framework for exploring the shadow's role in our lives.

1. **The Hero and the Shadow**

   The hero archetype embodies courage, determination, and growth, but no hero is complete without a shadow. The shadow is the hero's adversary and often represents their deepest fears or unacknowledged weaknesses. This dynamic is evident in the Star Wars saga, where Luke Skywalker must confront Darth Vader—his literal and figurative shadow.

2. **The Anima and Animus**

   The anima (feminine aspect of the male psyche) and animus (masculine aspect of the female psyche) represent the shadowed, repressed elements of gender identity. Myths often explore these archetypes through figures like Aphrodite (anima) or Ares (animus), encouraging balance and integration.

3. **The Shadow Archetype**

   The shadow archetype encompasses all the qualities we deny in ourselves. It is often portrayed in myths as monsters, villains, or dark gods, such as Hades or Kali. By acknowledging and integrating the shadow archetype, we access a reservoir of creative and transformative energy.

4. **The Wise Old Man and the Mentor**

   Archetypes like the Wise Old Man or Mentor (e.g., Merlin, Yoda, or Gandalf) often guide the hero in understanding and integrating the shadow. These figures symbolize the wisdom gained from embracing the entirety of the self.

The Shadow's Role in Personal Myths

The myths we live by—the narratives we tell ourselves about who we are and what our lives mean—are deeply influenced by the shadow. If left unexplored, the shadow can distort these personal myths, leading to self-limiting beliefs or behaviors. Recognizing and addressing the shadow within our narratives allows us to rewrite our stories and reclaim our power.

1. **Identifying Shadow Influences in Personal Myths**
   Consider how your personal myths reflect unacknowledged fears or desires. For instance, a narrative of "I'm not good enough" may stem from the shadow's internalized voice of past criticism or failure. By identifying these influences, you can challenge and reshape them.
2. **Integrating the Shadow into Your Myth**
   Integration doesn't mean erasing the shadow but incorporating its lessons. A narrative of "I'm not good enough" might evolve into "I am capable, even when I face challenges," transforming a limiting belief into one of empowerment.

Mythology as a Guide to Shadow Integration

Myths offer symbolic maps for navigating the shadow. They teach us that the journey into darkness is not an end but a means to transformation. By engaging with mythological symbols and stories, we can gain insights into our inner worlds and apply them to our lives.

1. **Creating Your Mythic Journey**
   Begin by envisioning yourself as the hero of your story. Identify the shadow elements you must confront—these might appear as challenges, fears, or recurring patterns. Use mythic imagery to frame your journey, imagining your shadow as a dragon, labyrinth, or underworld to explore.
2. **Ritual and Symbolism**
   Engage with myths through rituals or symbolic acts. For example, lighting a candle to symbolize bringing light to the shadow, or journaling as a way of mapping your internal underworld, can make the abstract process of shadow integration tangible and meaningful.

Lessons from Mythology: Embracing Complexity

The enduring appeal of mythology lies in its ability to hold complexity. Myths remind us that light and dark are not opposites but interconnected forces. The hero is not truly heroic without the challenges of the shadow. By embracing this duality, we learn to accept ourselves more fully.

Shadow work, like mythology, is a journey that requires courage, curiosity, and a willingness to confront the unknown. In the next chapter, we will delve deeper into the practical tools and techniques that will help you integrate the lessons of mythology and archetypes into your personal shadowplay. But for now, let the stories of the past inspire you to face the shadows of your present, knowing that every step into the darkness brings you closer to the light.

Chapter 3: Jungian Shadows: A Psychological Perspective

Carl Jung's exploration of the human psyche revolutionized how we understand the complexities of the self. At the heart of Jungian psychology lies the concept of the shadow, a term he used to describe the hidden, unconscious parts of ourselves. These are the aspects we suppress, deny, or fail to recognize, often because they conflict with our conscious self-image or societal expectations. This chapter delves into the Jungian perspective on shadows, exploring their formation, role in psychological development, and how engaging with them can lead to personal transformation and wholeness.

The Shadow in Jungian Psychology: An Overview

Jung described the shadow as the "dark side" of the psyche, though he emphasized that it is not inherently negative. The shadow contains everything outside the conscious awareness, including traits and emotions we might consider undesirable, as well as latent talents and untapped potential. It represents the parts of ourselves we avoid confronting, either because they contradict our ideal self or because we fear their implications.

Characteristics of the Shadow:

- **Unconscious Nature**: The shadow operates outside conscious awareness, influencing our behaviors and emotions in ways we might not recognize.
- **Dual Nature**: While often associated with negative traits like anger or jealousy, the shadow also houses positive qualities we fail to acknowledge, such as creativity, resilience, or assertiveness.
- **Projection**: The shadow frequently manifests through projection, where we attribute our hidden traits to others, seeing in them what we deny in ourselves.

How the Shadow Is Formed

The shadow begins to develop early in life as we learn to navigate social and cultural norms. As children, we are encouraged to adopt behaviors that align with societal expectations and suppress those deemed unacceptable. This process of socialization creates a divide between the conscious self (the persona) and the unconscious shadow.

Key Factors in Shadow Formation:

1. **Cultural and Societal Norms**

   Cultural values dictate what is considered "good" or "bad," shaping what aspects of ourselves we suppress. For example, societies that prioritize emotional stoicism might encourage individuals to repress feelings of vulnerability or sadness.

2. **Parental Influence**

   Parents, caregivers, and authority figures reinforce behaviors they deem acceptable, often unconsciously teaching children to hide or deny other parts of themselves.

3. **Personal Experiences**

   Traumatic events, failures, or rejections can lead us to bury traits or emotions associated with those experiences, deepening the shadow.

4. **Ego Development**

   The ego, our conscious sense of identity, seeks to maintain a cohesive and positive self-image. Traits that threaten this image are relegated to the shadow.

The Role of the Shadow in Psychological Development

While the shadow is often seen as a source of conflict, Jung believed it plays a crucial role in personal growth and individuation—a process he described as becoming the most authentic version of oneself. The shadow, when engaged with consciously, offers a path to self-awareness and integration.

Functions of the Shadow:

1. **Revealing Hidden Truths**

   The shadow acts as a mirror, reflecting the aspects of ourselves we need to confront to grow. By acknowledging these truths, we gain deeper insight into our motivations and behaviors.

2. **Challenging the Ego**

   The shadow challenges the ego's need for control and perfection, teaching us to embrace imperfection and complexity.

3. **Unlocking Creativity**

   The shadow often contains repressed creative energy. Artists, writers, and innovators frequently tap into their shadow to access profound inspiration and originality.

4. **Driving Transformation**

   Confronting the shadow requires courage and honesty, but it ultimately leads to greater self-acceptance and psychological resilience.

The Dangers of Ignoring the Shadow

Ignoring the shadow does not make it disappear; it amplifies its influence. When left unchecked, the shadow can manifest in destructive ways, both internally and externally.

Consequences of Suppressing the Shadow:

1. **Projection**

   Unacknowledged shadow traits are often projected onto others, leading to misunderstandings, conflicts, and prejudice. For example, someone who denies their own ambition might resent or criticize others who are driven.

2. **Emotional Repression**

   Suppressed emotions can lead to psychological and physical stress, manifesting as anxiety, depression, or chronic health issues.

3. **Self-Sabotage**

   The shadow can unconsciously influence decisions, creating patterns of self-sabotage or recurring life challenges.

4. **Fragmentation**

   Denying the shadow creates a sense of inner division, preventing individuals from feeling whole or authentic.

Engaging with the Shadow: Jungian Shadow Work

Jung believed that shadow integration is essential for personal growth. Shadow work involves bringing unconscious elements into conscious awareness, allowing us to confront, understand, and integrate them.

Steps in Shadow Work:

1. **Recognition**

   The first step is recognizing the shadow's presence. Pay attention to emotional triggers, recurring patterns, or traits you judge harshly in others—these often point to shadow elements.

2. **Reflection**

   Reflect on your personal history to uncover the origins of shadow traits. Journaling, therapy, or meditative practices can help explore these hidden aspects.

3. **Acceptance**

   Shadow work requires compassion and nonjudgment. Accepting the shadow does not mean endorsing harmful behaviors but understanding the emotions and motivations behind them.

4. **Integration**

   Integration involves finding a balanced expression of shadow traits. For instance, channeling repressed anger into assertiveness or transforming envy into inspiration.

Tools and Practices for Shadow Work

Several techniques can aid in exploring and integrating the shadow, many of which align with Jung's teachings:

1. **Active Imagination**

   This Jungian technique involves engaging with the subconscious through visualization or dialogue. Imagine conversing with your shadow, asking it questions to understand its perspective.

2. **Dream Analysis**

   Dreams often reveal shadow elements through symbolic imagery. Keep a dream journal and reflect on recurring themes or characters.

3. **Creative Expression**

   Art, writing, and other creative outlets can provide a safe space to explore and express shadow aspects.

4. **Therapeutic Support**

   Working with a Jungian therapist or counselor can provide guidance and structure for shadow work.

5. **Mindfulness and Meditation**

   Mindfulness practices create a nonjudgmental space for observing thoughts and emotions, facilitating awareness of the shadow.

Shadow Integration: The Path to Wholeness

Jung emphasized that the goal of shadow work is not to eliminate the shadow but to integrate it into the self. Integration brings balance, enabling us to harness the shadow's energy and wisdom without being controlled by it. This process of individuation allows us to move beyond the dualities of light and dark, embracing the complexity and totality of who we are.

In the journey toward individuation, the shadow becomes an ally rather than an adversary—a guide to greater self-awareness and authenticity. By engaging with the shadow, we cultivate resilience, creativity, and compassion, both for ourselves and for others.

As we continue to explore the themes of shadowplay in this book, remember that the shadow is not something to fear but a vital part of your inner landscape. It is through the shadow that we find the light, and it is through understanding ourselves that we unlock the potential for true transformation.

Chapter 4: The Hero's Journey: Understanding Your Mythic Path

The Hero's Journey, a concept popularized by mythologist Joseph Campbell, serves as a universal blueprint for personal growth and transformation. Found in myths, legends, and stories across cultures, this archetypal journey reflects the trials, triumphs, and self-discovery that shape every human life. In this chapter, we will explore the stages of the Hero's Journey, its psychological significance, and how you can use this framework to understand your own mythic path. By seeing your life through the lens of this timeless structure, you can uncover new meaning, overcome challenges, and align with your highest potential.

The Hero's Journey: A Universal Blueprint

Campbell introduced the Hero's Journey in his seminal work *The Hero with a Thousand Faces*, identifying recurring patterns in myths from around the world. These patterns form a narrative arc that begins with a call to adventure, leads through trials and tribulations, and culminates in transformation and return. The Hero's Journey is not limited to fictional tales—it is a metaphor for the psychological and spiritual journey each of us undertakes.

Key Characteristics of the Hero's Journey:

- **Universality**: Found in cultures across the globe, the Hero's Journey resonates with the shared human experience.
- **Symbolism**: Each stage represents psychological or spiritual challenges we face in life.
- **Cyclic Nature**: The journey is not linear but cyclical, reflecting the ongoing nature of growth and self-discovery.

The Stages of the Hero's Journey

The Hero's Journey typically unfolds in three main acts: **Departure**, **Initiation**, and **Return**. Each act contains distinct stages that mirror the challenges and milestones of personal transformation.

Act 1: Departure (Separation from the Known World)

1. **The Ordinary World**
   This is where the hero begins their journey, living a life that feels familiar but incomplete. It represents the comfort zone, where fears and doubts often keep us stagnant. For example, in *The Hobbit*, Bilbo Baggins starts in the Shire, content but unfulfilled.

2. **The Call to Adventure**
   A challenge, opportunity, or disruption invites the hero to leave their ordinary world. The call can be external (a crisis or event) or internal (a yearning for change). This moment signifies the awakening of the hero's potential.

3. **Refusal of the Call**
   The hero often hesitates, fearing the unknown or doubting their abilities. This stage reflects the resistance we all feel when faced with change.

4. **Meeting the Mentor**

   A guide or teacher appears, offering wisdom, tools, or encouragement to help the hero embark on their journey. In mythology, this mentor might be a wise elder, a magical being, or even a symbolic object.

5. **Crossing the Threshold**

   The hero commits to the journey, stepping into the unknown. This marks the beginning of transformation as the hero leaves behind the familiar world.

Act 2: Initiation (The Trials of Transformation)

1. **Tests, Allies, and Enemies**

   In this stage, the hero encounters challenges, builds alliances, and confronts adversaries. These trials test their strength, resilience, and values, teaching important lessons. Symbolically, this is where the shadow often emerges, forcing the hero to confront hidden fears or flaws.

2. **The Approach to the Inmost Cave**

   The hero journeys inward, preparing to face their greatest challenge. The "cave" represents the depths of the subconscious or a life-defining trial that must be overcome.

3. **The Ordeal**

   The hero faces a climactic confrontation, often risking everything. This moment of crisis symbolizes death and rebirth, a shedding of the old self to make way for transformation.

4. **The Reward (Seizing the Sword)**

   Having overcome the ordeal, the hero gains a reward, insight, or newfound power. This "sword" can be a literal or metaphorical tool that equips the hero for the final phase of their journey.

Act 3: Return (Integration and Sharing the Gift)

1. **The Road Back**

   The hero begins the journey home, integrating their newfound wisdom or power into their life. This stage often presents new challenges, testing the hero's ability to hold onto their transformation.

2. **The Resurrection**

   The hero undergoes a final test, symbolizing ultimate transformation. This rebirth allows the hero to transcend their former limitations and embody their truest self.

3. **Return with the Elixir**

   The hero returns to their ordinary world, bringing the "elixir"—a gift of wisdom, healing, or empowerment. They share this gift with others, completing the cycle of growth and service.

The Psychological Significance of the Hero's Journey

The Hero's Journey is not just a narrative structure; it is a profound psychological framework that mirrors the process of individuation described by Carl Jung. Each stage of the journey corresponds to challenges and transformations in the human psyche.

1. **The Call to Adventure as Awakening**
   The call represents an inner yearning for change or growth, often triggered by life events or personal crises.
2. **Tests and Trials as Shadow Work**
   The trials the hero faces symbolize encounters with the shadow, requiring self-awareness and courage to overcome.
3. **The Ordeal as Transformation**
   The ordeal represents a death-and-rebirth cycle, mirroring psychological breakthroughs where the old self gives way to a more authentic self.
4. **The Return as Integration**
   Returning with the elixir signifies the integration of new insights, skills, or wisdom into daily life, fostering wholeness and balance.

Crafting Your Own Hero's Journey

By viewing your life through the lens of the Hero's Journey, you can transform challenges into opportunities for growth. Reflect on your experiences and identify the stages of your personal journey.

1. **Identify Your Ordinary World**
   What is your current comfort zone? What aspects of your life feel stagnant or unfulfilling?
2. **Recognize Your Call to Adventure**
   What opportunities or challenges are inviting you to grow? What fears or doubts are holding you back?
3. **Confront Your Threshold Guardians**
   What external or internal barriers are preventing you from moving forward? How can you overcome them?
4. **Engage with Mentors and Allies**
   Who are the mentors, friends, or resources that can guide and support you on your journey?
5. **Prepare for the Ordeal**
   What is the greatest challenge you face? How can you equip yourself mentally, emotionally, or spiritually to confront it?
6. **Claim Your Reward and Share It**
   What wisdom or strength have you gained from your journey? How can you use it to enrich your life and the lives of others?

Lessons from the Hero's Journey

The Hero's Journey teaches us that life's challenges are not obstacles to avoid but essential steps on the path to growth. By embracing the journey, we learn to navigate uncertainty, confront our fears, and emerge stronger and wiser. It reminds us that transformation is not a destination but a continuous process, and that each of us has the capacity to become the hero of our own story.

As you continue to explore shadowplay and personal mythology, keep the Hero's Journey in mind as a guide. The challenges you face, the allies you meet, and the lessons you learn all contribute to your unique mythic path. And with each cycle of the journey, you move closer to embodying your fullest potential.

Chapter 5: Light and Dark: Duality in Personal Growth

Life is a dance of opposites—light and dark, joy and sorrow, strength and vulnerability. In this eternal interplay lies the essence of personal growth. The duality of light and dark shapes not only the external world but also our internal landscapes. To embrace growth is to navigate this duality, acknowledging both the luminous and shadowed parts of our existence.

In this chapter, we will explore the concept of duality, its role in self-discovery, and how integrating light and dark can lead to profound transformation. By understanding the symbiotic relationship between opposites, you can cultivate balance, authenticity, and a deeper connection to your true self.

The Nature of Duality: Opposites in Harmony

Duality is the principle that opposites coexist and depend on each other for meaning. Light has no significance without darkness, just as joy cannot be understood without sadness. In many spiritual and philosophical traditions, duality is seen as the fundamental structure of existence.

Examples of Duality in Nature and Culture:

- **Day and Night**: The cycle of light and dark governs the natural world, symbolizing renewal and rest.
- **Yin and Yang**: In Taoism, yin represents the feminine, receptive, and dark, while yang symbolizes the masculine, active, and light. Together, they form a harmonious whole.
- **Life and Death**: The cycle of birth and death underscores the transient nature of existence, encouraging acceptance of both beginnings and endings.

In the context of personal growth, duality reflects the interplay between our conscious and unconscious selves, strengths and weaknesses, and aspirations and fears. Growth arises not by favoring one side over the other but by finding balance and integration.

Light: The Conscious Self and Its Aspirations

Light symbolizes awareness, clarity, and the qualities we strive to embody. It represents the aspects of ourselves that align with societal ideals and personal goals.

Characteristics of Light:

- **Conscious Awareness**: Light encompasses what we are aware of, including our strengths, talents, and values.
- **Aspiration and Growth**: It reflects our desire for improvement, success, and fulfillment.
- **Empathy and Connection**: Light fosters compassion, kindness, and the ability to form meaningful relationships.

While the light is often associated with positivity, it can also create challenges. Over-identification with light can lead to perfectionism, denial of vulnerability, and the suppression of authentic emotions. When we focus solely on the light, we risk ignoring the depth and richness that comes from embracing our shadows.

Dark: The Unconscious Self and Its Depths

Darkness, often misunderstood or feared, represents the unknown, the hidden, and the repressed. It is the domain of the shadow self, containing both the traits we disown and the untapped potential waiting to be discovered.

Characteristics of Darkness:

- **The Shadow Self**: The dark includes our unacknowledged fears, insecurities, and desires.
- **Creativity and Mystery**: Darkness is a source of imagination and intuition, offering insights that cannot be accessed through logic alone.
- **Transformation**: Like seeds that germinate in the dark, personal growth often begins in moments of uncertainty, struggle, or introspection.

Engaging with the dark can be uncomfortable, but it is essential for self-discovery. The shadow, when integrated, becomes a wellspring of resilience, authenticity, and creativity.

The Interplay of Light and Dark in Personal Growth

Personal growth is not about eliminating darkness or striving for perpetual light; it is about balancing and integrating both. The tension between opposites creates opportunities for transformation and wholeness.

Key Insights into Their Relationship:

1. **Light Illuminates the Dark**

   Conscious awareness (light) helps us recognize and confront unconscious patterns (darkness). This process transforms fear into understanding.

2. **Darkness Grounds the Light**

   Engaging with the shadow prevents us from becoming ungrounded or overly idealistic. It connects us to our humanity and authenticity.

3. **The Middle Path**

   Growth lies in the "gray areas" where light and dark intersect. This middle ground fosters acceptance, compassion, and balance.

Tools for Integrating Light and Dark

The integration of light and dark requires self-awareness, curiosity, and a willingness to embrace complexity. Here are practical tools to navigate this duality:

1. **Shadow Work**
   - **Journaling**: Write about traits or emotions you find difficult to accept in yourself. Reflect on their origins and how they influence your behavior.
   - **Projection Analysis**: Notice qualities you judge in others. These may reflect unacknowledged aspects of your shadow.
2. **Gratitude and Acceptance Practices**
   - Celebrate your strengths while acknowledging your imperfections. Gratitude for both light and dark experiences cultivates resilience and self-acceptance.
3. **Creative Expression**
   - Use art, music, or storytelling to explore both the luminous and shadowed parts of yourself. Creativity bridges the conscious and unconscious.
4. **Mindfulness and Meditation**
   - Practice mindfulness to observe your thoughts and emotions without judgment. This creates space for both light and dark to coexist.
5. **Rituals and Symbols**
   - Engage with symbolic acts, such as lighting a candle in a dark room, to honor the interplay between opposites.
6. **Therapeutic Support**
   - Work with a therapist or coach trained in shadow integration to navigate challenging emotions or patterns.

Stories of Light and Dark: Mythic Lessons

Myths and stories often illustrate the dynamic interplay between light and dark. Heroes who ignore their shadows fail, while those who embrace both succeed. Consider these examples:

- **The Balance in Harry Potter**: Harry's strength comes not from rejecting his connection to Voldemort (darkness) but from accepting it and choosing a different path (light).
- **The Redemption of Darth Vader**: In *Star Wars*, Darth Vader's arc demonstrates the transformative power of acknowledging one's shadow and choosing to return to the light.
- **The Duality of Persephone**: As the queen of the Underworld and goddess of spring, Persephone embodies the coexistence of life and death, light and dark.

These stories remind us that duality is not a flaw but a fundamental aspect of existence.

The Rewards of Embracing Duality

When we embrace light and dark, we unlock the potential for:

- **Authenticity**: Living in alignment with our true selves, free from denial or pretense.
- **Resilience**: Gaining strength from both triumphs and challenges.
- **Compassion**: Understanding that everyone, including ourselves, carries both light and shadow.
- **Wisdom**: Drawing insights from the full spectrum of human experience.

Moving Forward: Duality as a Guide

As you continue your journey of personal growth, view light and dark as allies rather than adversaries. Each has unique lessons to offer, and together they form the foundation for a rich, balanced, and meaningful life. The goal is not to "fix" yourself by eliminating flaws but to embrace the complexity of your humanity.

In the chapters ahead, we will delve deeper into specific practices and stories that illuminate the path to integrating light and dark. For now, reflect on the ways duality manifests in your life and consider how you might bring these opposites into greater harmony. True transformation lies not in choosing one over the other but in embracing the dance of both.

Part 2: Exploring Your Shadow

Chapter 6: Identifying Your Shadow: Tools and Techniques

The shadow—the hidden, unconscious part of your psyche—shapes your thoughts, emotions, and behaviors in ways you may not fully realize. It influences how you view yourself, interact with others, and navigate the world. Identifying your shadow is the first step toward integrating it into your conscious awareness, transforming it from a disruptive force into a source of insight and growth.

This chapter provides an extensive guide to understanding the signs of your shadow, recognizing its manifestations, and employing effective tools and techniques for shadow identification. By the end of this chapter, you'll have a clear roadmap to begin uncovering and engaging with your shadow.

Why Identify Your Shadow?

Before exploring the methods to identify your shadow, it's essential to understand why this process matters. The shadow operates in the background of your psyche, influencing your reactions, choices, and relationships without your conscious consent. Ignoring it can lead to emotional distress, unresolved conflicts, and repetitive patterns. Engaging with the shadow offers several benefits:

- **Self-Awareness**: You gain a deeper understanding of your behaviors, triggers, and motivations.
- **Healing**: Uncovering suppressed emotions allows you to process and release them.
- **Personal Growth**: Shadow work fosters authenticity, creativity, and resilience.
- **Improved Relationships**: Recognizing and owning your projections reduces conflict and deepens connections with others.

Recognizing the Signs of Your Shadow

Your shadow doesn't announce itself overtly—it often reveals its presence through subtle or unconscious patterns. Here are some common ways the shadow manifests:

1. **Emotional Triggers**

   Strong, disproportionate emotional reactions to people or situations often indicate shadow elements. For example, if arrogance in others angers you, it might reflect suppressed pride or insecurity within yourself.

2. **Repetitive Patterns**

   Recurring challenges in relationships, career, or personal goals often point to unresolved shadow issues. These patterns are opportunities to confront hidden beliefs or fears.

3. **Projection onto Others**

   The traits you dislike or admire in others can reveal aspects of your shadow. Projection occurs when you attribute your repressed qualities to someone else, seeing in them what you cannot acknowledge in yourself.

4. **Feelings of Guilt or Shame**

   Persistent guilt or shame may stem from shadow elements you were taught to reject, such as ambition, anger, or sensuality.

5. **Self-Sabotage**

   Behaviors that undermine your success or happiness—like procrastination, addiction, or perfectionism—often originate from unexamined shadow aspects.

6. **Dream Symbols**

   Dreams frequently depict shadow elements through symbols, recurring themes, or characters. Pay attention to dark, mysterious, or threatening figures in your dreams.

Tools and Techniques for Shadow Identification

The process of identifying your shadow involves turning inward and bringing unconscious aspects of yourself into awareness. Below are proven tools and techniques to help you explore your shadow:

1. Self-Reflection and Journaling

Journaling is one of the most effective ways to uncover your shadow. It allows you to explore your thoughts and emotions in a structured yet open-ended manner.

Prompts for Shadow Exploration:

- What traits or behaviors in others irritate or anger me? Why?
- When do I feel ashamed, guilty, or embarrassed?
- What patterns or challenges keep repeating in my life?
- What compliments make me uncomfortable?
- What is something I secretly envy in others?

Use these questions to write freely, allowing insights to emerge without judgment.

2. Projection Analysis

Projection is a natural psychological defense mechanism that reveals shadow elements by externalizing them. To identify projections, ask yourself:

- Who do I admire, envy, or resent deeply?
- What qualities in others provoke a strong emotional response in me?
- Could these traits reflect something I dislike—or secretly value—in myself?

For instance, if you find someone's confidence off-putting, it may indicate suppressed feelings of inadequacy or a longing to express confidence yourself.

3. Dream Work

Dreams serve as a direct line to the unconscious, often dramatizing shadow elements through symbols and narratives. To analyze your dreams:

- **Keep a Dream Journal**: Record your dreams immediately upon waking, noting recurring symbols, characters, or emotions.
- **Identify Themes**: Look for patterns or recurring imagery that evoke strong feelings.
- **Reflect on Dream Characters**: Each character may represent an aspect of yourself, including shadow traits.

For example, encountering an antagonist in a dream could symbolize a part of you that you've been resisting or denying.

4. Mindfulness and Meditation

Mindfulness practices create space for observing thoughts and emotions without judgment, allowing shadow elements to surface.

Meditation Techniques for Shadow Work:

- **Inner Observation**: Sit in silence and observe your thoughts, paying attention to recurring themes or emotions.
- **Guided Visualizations**: Use visualizations to meet your shadow. Imagine yourself descending into a symbolic "underworld" to confront and understand hidden aspects of yourself.
- **Body Awareness**: Notice where emotions manifest physically, such as tension in the shoulders or a pit in the stomach. These sensations can provide clues to shadow elements.

5. Artistic Expression

Art, music, and other creative outlets offer a safe space to explore your shadow through symbolic representation.

Artistic Exercises:

- **Drawing or Painting**: Create abstract or literal depictions of your emotions, fears, or recurring dreams.
- **Writing Fiction**: Develop characters or stories that embody traits you find difficult to accept in yourself.
- **Music and Dance**: Use music or movement to express repressed emotions or explore themes of duality.

6. Therapeutic Techniques

Working with a therapist trained in shadow work or Jungian psychology can provide a structured and supportive environment for exploring the shadow. Techniques may include:

- **Active Imagination**: A Jungian method where you engage in dialogue with aspects of your unconscious, such as shadow figures, during a meditative state.
- **Somatic Therapy**: Focusing on bodily sensations to uncover suppressed emotions and memories.
- **Cognitive Behavioral Therapy (CBT)**: Identifying and challenging thought patterns that stem from shadow influences.

7. Archetype Exploration

Archetypes are universal symbols found in myths and stories that reflect aspects of the human experience. Engaging with archetypes can help you identify shadow traits.

Steps to Explore Archetypes:

- Reflect on which archetypes resonate with or repel you (e.g., The Rebel, The Lover, The Sage).
- Identify traits within these archetypes that align with your shadow.
- Use journaling or visualization to explore how these archetypes influence your life.

Practical Example: Identifying a Shadow Trait

Imagine you frequently feel irritated by people who are overly assertive. Using the tools outlined:

1. **Self-Reflection**: Journaling reveals that you were taught as a child to prioritize others' needs, leading you to suppress your own assertiveness.
2. **Projection Analysis**: Recognize that your irritation stems from envy or discomfort with your own repressed desire to set boundaries.
3. **Dream Work**: A recent dream of a loud, commanding figure may represent your suppressed assertiveness trying to emerge.
4. **Creative Expression**: Draw or write about the emotions triggered by assertive individuals, exploring how they relate to your inner world.

Through this process, you begin to reclaim your assertiveness, transforming it from a source of discomfort into a tool for personal empowerment.

Overcoming Resistance to Shadow Work

Shadow work can be uncomfortable, as it involves confronting parts of yourself you may prefer to ignore. Common resistances include fear, denial, or judgment. To overcome these barriers:

- **Practice Self-Compassion**: Approach shadow work with kindness and curiosity rather than self-criticism.
- **Take Small Steps**: Start with manageable practices, such as journaling or reflecting on a single emotional trigger.
- **Seek Support**: Share your experiences with a trusted friend, mentor, or therapist.

Moving Forward: A Commitment to Self-Discovery

Identifying your shadow is an ongoing journey rather than a one-time achievement. Each layer you uncover brings you closer to authenticity and wholeness. As you engage with the tools and techniques in this chapter, remember that the shadow is not an adversary but an integral part of who you are. By bringing it into the light, you reclaim your power and unlock the potential for profound personal transformation.

Chapter 7: Emotional Mapping: Connecting Feelings to Shadows

Emotions are a powerful gateway to the shadow self. They provide clues about our unconscious patterns, suppressed desires, and hidden fears. By understanding and mapping our emotional responses, we can uncover the shadow's influence in our lives and begin the process of integration. Emotional mapping is a technique that links feelings to shadow traits, enabling us to identify unresolved issues and patterns.

This chapter explores the art of emotional mapping, its significance in shadow work, and the step-by-step process to connect your emotions to shadow aspects. By the end of this chapter, you will have the tools to recognize, understand, and work through emotional triggers with greater awareness and compassion.

The Role of Emotions in Shadow Work

Emotions act as signals from the unconscious, drawing our attention to areas that require healing or acknowledgment. When we suppress or deny parts of ourselves, those parts do not disappear—they manifest as emotional reactions.

Common Emotional Indicators of Shadow Traits:

1. **Anger**: Often linked to repressed boundaries, unmet needs, or unresolved pain.
2. **Jealousy**: May point to unacknowledged desires or feelings of inadequacy.
3. **Guilt or Shame**: Reflects internalized societal or familial judgments about "unacceptable" traits.
4. **Fear**: Signals hidden insecurities, unresolved trauma, or avoidance of growth.
5. **Sadness**: Can be a response to suppressed grief, unexpressed emotions, or a sense of loss.

By paying attention to these emotions, you gain insight into the aspects of your shadow that are seeking recognition.

What Is Emotional Mapping?

Emotional mapping is the process of identifying, analyzing, and linking your emotions to specific shadow traits or patterns. This technique allows you to visualize the connections between your feelings, behaviors, and unconscious influences, providing clarity and a path toward integration.

Benefits of Emotional Mapping:

- **Self-Awareness**: Understand why you feel the way you do in specific situations.
- **Pattern Recognition**: Identify recurring emotional triggers and their roots.
- **Empowerment**: Transform emotional reactivity into conscious choice and action.
- **Healing**: Address and integrate suppressed emotions, fostering psychological and emotional well-being.

The Emotional Mapping Process

The process of emotional mapping involves several steps, from recognizing triggers to uncovering shadow traits. Here's a comprehensive guide:

Step 1: Identify Emotional Triggers

The first step in emotional mapping is to recognize the situations, people, or environments that evoke strong emotional reactions. Triggers often point to unresolved issues or shadow traits.

Common Examples of Triggers:

- Feeling defensive during criticism.
- Experiencing envy when someone achieves success.
- Reacting with anger to perceived unfairness.
- Avoiding situations that evoke anxiety or fear.

Exercise:

Keep a trigger journal for a week. Write down instances where you felt a strong emotional reaction, noting:

- The situation.
- The people involved.
- The emotion(s) you experienced.

Step 2: Examine the Emotion

Once you've identified a trigger, analyze the emotion it evokes. Ask yourself:

- What am I feeling? (e.g., anger, sadness, shame)
- How intense is this emotion?
- Is this a recurring emotion in similar situations?

Exercise:

Use a feelings wheel or chart to pinpoint your emotions. This can help you move beyond broad labels like "angry" or "sad" to more specific descriptors like "frustrated" or "lonely."

Step 3: Explore the Underlying Cause

Every emotion has a root cause, often tied to unmet needs, unresolved conflicts, or suppressed traits. Reflect on why the trigger evoked such a strong reaction.

Questions for Reflection:

1. What does this emotion remind me of? (e.g., past experiences or relationships)
2. What need or value feels violated in this situation?
3. Could this emotion reflect something I've suppressed in myself?

Example:

If you feel anger when someone takes credit for your work, the underlying cause might be a suppressed need for recognition or a fear of being overlooked.

Step 4: Connect to Shadow Traits

Once you've explored the root cause, link the emotion to potential shadow traits. Consider:

- Is this a trait I dislike or deny in myself?
- Could this emotion reflect something I fear to express?
- Does this connect to a past experience where I suppressed this part of myself?

Exercise:

Create a list of shadow traits that might be connected to your recurring emotions. For instance:

- **Anger**: Linked to suppressed assertiveness or fear of vulnerability.
- **Jealousy**: Connected to unacknowledged ambition or self-doubt.
- **Guilt**: Stemming from internalized perfectionism or fear of failure.

Step 5: Map the Connections

Visualize the relationships between your triggers, emotions, and shadow traits. This step helps you see patterns and provides a clear roadmap for shadow integration.

How to Create an Emotional Map:

1. Write your triggers in a central column.
2. To the left, list the emotions each trigger evokes.
3. To the right, list the shadow traits connected to those emotions.

Example:

Trigger	Emotion	Shadow Trait
Criticized at work	Anger	Fear of inadequacy
Friend's promotion	Jealousy	Suppressed ambition
Forgetting an obligation	Guilt	Internalized perfectionism

Step 6: Reflect and Integrate

With your emotional map complete, reflect on how these connections influence your life and how you can begin integrating the shadow traits.

Key Reflection Questions:

- How has suppressing these traits affected my decisions or relationships?
- What can I learn from these emotions about myself?
- How can I express these traits in a healthy, balanced way?

Tools for Emotional Mapping

Several tools and practices can enhance your emotional mapping process:

1. **Journaling**: Write daily about your emotional experiences, focusing on triggers and their deeper meanings.
2. **Therapy**: Work with a therapist trained in shadow work or emotional processing to uncover hidden patterns.
3. **Meditation**: Practice mindfulness to observe emotions as they arise without judgment.
4. **Creative Expression**: Use art, music, or storytelling to explore and externalize complex emotions.

Practical Application: An Emotional Mapping Example

Scenario:

You feel intense resentment when a colleague is praised in a meeting.

Mapping Process:

1. **Trigger**: Colleague receives praise.
2. **Emotion**: Resentment and jealousy.
3. **Root Cause**: You feel undervalued and fear that your contributions are overlooked.
4. **Shadow Trait**: Suppressed need for recognition and fear of self-promotion.
5. **Reflection**: Recognize that your resentment stems from a denied desire to advocate for yourself.

Integration:

Practice healthy self-assertion by sharing your accomplishments with your team and seeking feedback from your manager.

The Role of Compassion in Emotional Mapping

Shadow work is not about blaming yourself for your emotions but approaching them with compassion and curiosity. Emotional mapping is an opportunity to understand yourself more deeply, honor your humanity, and transform unconscious patterns into conscious growth.

Moving Forward: Using Emotional Maps for Growth

Emotional mapping is a dynamic, ongoing process. As you continue to map your emotions, you will uncover deeper layers of your shadow and gain greater clarity about your inner world. This practice fosters emotional intelligence, resilience, and self-acceptance, equipping you to navigate life's challenges with greater awareness and authenticity.

Chapter 8: Confronting Inner Demons: Facing Fears and Flaws

Every journey of personal growth requires a confrontation with the inner demons that dwell within our psyche. These demons are not literal entities but symbolic representations of our deepest fears, unresolved traumas, and perceived flaws. They manifest as self-doubt, anxiety, shame, and limiting beliefs, often acting as barriers to self-actualization. Facing these inner demons is essential for integrating the shadow and unlocking our fullest potential.

This chapter will explore the origins of inner demons, the psychological mechanisms that sustain them, and practical techniques to confront and transform them. By addressing these hidden aspects of yourself, you can break free from their influence and cultivate greater self-awareness, resilience, and empowerment.

Understanding Inner Demons: What Are They?

Inner demons represent the unresolved and often repressed aspects of our psyche that challenge our sense of self-worth and security. They are the voices of doubt, fear, and criticism that arise from past experiences, social conditioning, and unmet emotional needs.

Common Types of Inner Demons:

1. **Fear of Failure**: A paralyzing dread of making mistakes or falling short of expectations.
2. **Imposter Syndrome**: Persistent feelings of inadequacy despite evidence of competence or success.
3. **Perfectionism**: The relentless pursuit of flawlessness, often driven by fear of judgment or rejection.
4. **Shame**: A deep sense of unworthiness or guilt stemming from past actions or perceived flaws.
5. **Fear of Vulnerability**: The belief that showing weakness or emotions will lead to rejection or harm.

The Origins of Inner Demons

Inner demons are not inherent; they are shaped by our experiences and internalized narratives. Understanding their origins can help demystify their power and provide insight into how to confront them.

Key Sources of Inner Demons:

1. **Childhood Conditioning**
   - Negative reinforcement, overly critical parenting, or traumatic events can instill beliefs about worthiness and capability.
   - For example, a child who is constantly criticized may grow up with a fear of failure.
2. **Societal Expectations**
   - Cultural norms and societal pressures often create unrealistic standards for success, beauty, and behavior, fueling feelings of inadequacy.
3. **Past Traumas**
   - Unresolved trauma can create emotional wounds that manifest as anxiety, mistrust, or fear.
4. **Self-Comparison**
   - Comparing oneself to others, especially in the age of social media, can exacerbate feelings of unworthiness.
5. **Repressed Shadow Traits**
   - Traits or desires we deny or suppress often resurface as inner demons, seeking acknowledgment and integration.

Why Confront Inner Demons?

Confronting inner demons is not about eradicating them but understanding and transforming them. These demons hold valuable lessons about our vulnerabilities, needs, and strengths.

Benefits of Facing Inner Demons:

- **Self-Awareness**: Gain clarity about your fears, triggers, and limiting beliefs.
- **Emotional Freedom**: Release the grip of unresolved emotions and patterns.
- **Resilience**: Build the capacity to navigate challenges with courage and confidence.
- **Authenticity**: Embrace your flaws and vulnerabilities as integral parts of your humanity.

Practical Techniques for Confronting Inner Demons

Facing inner demons requires courage, compassion, and persistence. Below are detailed techniques to help you confront and transform these hidden aspects of yourself.

1. Acknowledge and Name Your Demons

The first step in confronting inner demons is to recognize their presence and name them. This diminishes their power by bringing them into conscious awareness.

Exercise:

- Write a list of fears, doubts, or limiting beliefs that frequently arise in your thoughts.
- Give each one a name or identity (e.g., "The Critic," "The Perfectionist," "The Doubter").
- Reflect on how these demons influence your behavior and choices.

Example:

- Fear of failure → "The Taskmaster."
- Shame → "The Judge."

2. Understand the Root Cause

Inner demons often originate from specific experiences or patterns of thought. Identifying their root cause helps you address the underlying issue.

Reflection Questions:

- When did I first experience this fear or belief?
- What events or relationships reinforced it?
- How has this demon protected or hindered me?

Example:

A fear of vulnerability might stem from being ridiculed as a child for expressing emotions.

3. Engage in Dialogue with Your Demons

Inner demons are parts of your psyche that seek acknowledgment. Engaging in a compassionate dialogue allows you to understand their purpose and transform their influence.

Technique:

- Imagine sitting across from your inner demon in a safe, calm space.
- Ask it questions such as:
  - "Why are you here?"
  - "What are you trying to protect me from?"
  - "What do you need from me to feel at peace?"
- Listen to its responses without judgment.

Example:
Your "Perfectionist" might reveal that it's trying to protect you from criticism or failure.

4. Reframe the Narrative

Inner demons often thrive on distorted narratives about yourself or the world. Reframing these narratives can shift your perspective and reduce their power.

Steps for Reframing:

1. Identify the belief your demon perpetuates (e.g., "I'm not good enough").
2. Challenge the belief with evidence or alternative perspectives.
3. Replace the belief with a more empowering narrative (e.g., "I'm learning and growing, and that's enough").

5. Embrace Vulnerability and Imperfection

Inner demons often feed on the fear of vulnerability or imperfection. By embracing these aspects of yourself, you disarm their power.

Practice:

- Share a personal fear or flaw with someone you trust.
- Reflect on how being vulnerable strengthens your relationships and self-acceptance.
- Celebrate small acts of imperfection, such as trying something new without striving for mastery.

6. Use Visualization to Transform Demons

Visualization is a powerful tool for symbolically confronting and transforming inner demons.

Visualization Exercise:

1. Close your eyes and imagine your inner demon as a physical entity.
2. Observe its appearance, size, and demeanor.
3. Visualize yourself engaging with it—offering understanding, compassion, or even a symbolic gift (e.g., light, water, or a token of peace).
4. See the demon transform into a less intimidating or more integrated form.

Example:
A towering, menacing figure might shrink into a smaller, approachable guide.

7. Seek Support

Confronting inner demons can be challenging, and seeking support from others can provide valuable perspective and encouragement.

Options for Support:

- Work with a therapist or counselor trained in shadow work or trauma recovery.
- Join a support group to share experiences and gain insights.

- Lean on trusted friends or mentors for guidance and reassurance.

Case Study: Confronting the Fear of Failure
Scenario:
A high-performing individual avoids taking risks due to a paralyzing fear of failure.
Process:

1. **Acknowledge**: They name this fear "The Critic."
2. **Understand**: Through journaling, they trace this fear to a childhood experience of being harshly criticized for making mistakes.
3. **Dialogue**: In a guided visualization, they ask "The Critic" why it exists. It responds, "I want to protect you from feeling inadequate."
4. **Reframe**: They adopt a new belief: "Failure is a stepping stone to growth, not a reflection of my worth."
5. **Transform**: They visualize "The Critic" as a wise teacher offering constructive feedback instead of harsh judgment.

Outcome:
By integrating this fear, they begin to take calculated risks and embrace failure as part of their journey.

The Role of Compassion in Confronting Inner Demons
Confronting inner demons requires self-compassion. These demons often formed as protective mechanisms, and acknowledging their purpose fosters a sense of understanding rather than hostility.

Compassion Practices:

- Speak to yourself with kindness, as you would a close friend.
- Remind yourself that facing fears and flaws is a sign of strength, not weakness.
- Celebrate progress, no matter how small.

Moving Forward: A Lifelong Journey
Facing inner demons is not a one-time event but an ongoing process of self-discovery and growth. As you continue this journey, remember that these demons are not enemies—they are teachers, guiding you toward greater awareness and authenticity.

Chapter 9: Transforming Pain: Finding Wisdom in the Shadows

Pain is an inevitable part of the human experience, often perceived as something to avoid or overcome. Yet within pain lies a profound opportunity for growth and transformation. The shadows of our lives—our fears, failures, and losses—often hold the greatest wisdom. When we learn to confront and embrace our pain, we unlock its potential to guide us toward resilience, compassion, and self-awareness.

In this chapter, we will explore the process of transforming pain into wisdom. By understanding the nature of pain, recognizing its role in our lives, and employing techniques to engage with it constructively, you can transform even the darkest experiences into sources of insight and empowerment.

The Nature of Pain: A Catalyst for Growth

Pain serves as a signal, alerting us to areas in our lives that require attention or change. Whether physical, emotional, or spiritual, pain is an inherent part of being human. Instead of viewing pain as an enemy, we can reframe it as a guide—a teacher that helps us understand ourselves more deeply.

Key Aspects of Pain:

1. **Emotional Pain**: Stemming from grief, heartbreak, rejection, or disappointment, emotional pain often highlights unmet needs or unresolved wounds.
2. **Physical Pain**: While rooted in the body, physical pain can reveal emotional or psychological struggles.
3. **Existential Pain**: The discomfort of questioning life's purpose, grappling with mortality, or confronting uncertainty.

Pain's transformative power lies in its ability to disrupt complacency, prompting introspection and inspiring change.

The Role of Pain in Shadow Work

Pain is intricately tied to the shadow self. Repressed emotions, unresolved trauma, and unacknowledged aspects of our identity often manifest as pain. Engaging with pain through shadow work allows us to uncover its origins, address its root causes, and integrate its lessons.

Pain as a Shadow Signal:

- **Triggers**: Painful reactions to specific situations often point to shadow elements seeking acknowledgment.
- **Repetition**: Patterns of recurring pain suggest unresolved issues or beliefs that need to be addressed.
- **Resistance**: Avoidance of pain can amplify its intensity, whereas facing it diminishes its power.

Why Transform Pain?

Transforming pain is not about erasing or denying it but finding meaning and purpose within it. By engaging with pain constructively, you can:

1. **Gain Insight**: Understand the deeper causes and messages behind your pain.
2. **Develop Resilience**: Build strength and adaptability by navigating challenges.
3. **Foster Compassion**: Pain fosters empathy for yourself and others, deepening your connections.
4. **Cultivate Growth**: Pain often precedes significant personal and spiritual growth.

Steps to Transforming Pain: A Guide to Finding Wisdom

Transforming pain involves a deliberate and compassionate process of exploration, acceptance, and integration. Below are detailed steps to guide you through this journey:

Step 1: Acknowledge Your Pain

Transformation begins with acknowledgment. Denying or avoiding pain only prolongs its hold on you.

Practice:

- Sit quietly and bring your awareness to the pain you are experiencing, whether physical or emotional.
- Name the pain. For example: "I feel grief," "I feel shame," or "I feel physical discomfort."
- Accept its presence without judgment. Remind yourself that it's okay to feel this way.

Step 2: Understand the Source of Your Pain

Pain often stems from unmet needs, unresolved trauma, or limiting beliefs. Exploring its source can provide clarity and direction for healing.

Reflection Questions:

1. What triggered this pain?
2. Have I experienced similar pain in the past?
3. What unmet need or unresolved issue might this pain represent?
4. Is this pain connected to a belief I hold about myself or the world?

Example:

A recurring sense of loneliness may stem from an unhealed wound of abandonment in childhood.

Step 3: Reframe Pain as a Teacher

Reframing pain shifts your perspective, allowing you to see it as a source of wisdom rather than an obstacle.

Exercise:

- Ask your pain: "What are you trying to teach me?"
- Write down any insights or messages that arise, even if they seem unclear at first.
- Reflect on how this pain might inspire growth, change, or self-discovery.

Step 4: Express Your Pain

Unexpressed pain often intensifies over time. Creative expression provides an outlet for releasing and processing painful emotions.

Methods for Expression:

- **Journaling**: Write about your pain, its impact on your life, and what you've learned from it.
- **Art**: Paint, draw, or sculpt to symbolize your pain and transformation.
- **Movement**: Use dance, yoga, or other physical activities to release stored tension.
- **Storytelling**: Share your experiences with a trusted friend or in a supportive group setting.

Step 5: Practice Self-Compassion

Pain can evoke harsh self-criticism or feelings of inadequacy. Practicing self-compassion helps you approach your pain with kindness and understanding.

Self-Compassion Practices:

1. **Self-Talk**: Speak to yourself as you would a dear friend. For example: "It's okay to feel this way. I'm here for you."
2. **Mindfulness**: Observe your pain without attaching to it or letting it define you.
3. **Affirmations**: Use affirmations such as "I am worthy of love and healing" or "This pain will pass."

Step 6: Find Meaning in Pain

Finding meaning in pain involves recognizing how it has shaped you and what it has taught you.

Reflection Questions:

1. How has this pain changed me or my perspective?
2. What strengths or insights have I gained from enduring this pain?
3. How can I use this experience to help myself or others?

Example:

Surviving a difficult breakup might teach you the importance of self-worth and set the stage for healthier relationships in the future.

Step 7: Integrate the Lessons

Transformation is complete when you integrate the lessons from your pain into your daily life. This integration turns pain into wisdom and ensures that it no longer holds power over you.

Steps for Integration:

1. Reflect on how you can apply the lessons learned to your current life.
2. Set intentions to act in alignment with these lessons (e.g., setting boundaries, pursuing passions, or prioritizing self-care).
3. Celebrate your progress and resilience, no matter how small.

Techniques for Transforming Pain

Here are additional techniques to support your journey:

1. **Meditation**: Use guided meditations focused on healing and self-compassion to connect with and soothe your pain.
2. **Inner Child Work**: Revisit painful childhood experiences with compassion to heal unresolved wounds.
3. **Rituals**: Create symbolic acts of release, such as writing down your pain and burning the paper as a gesture of letting go.
4. **Therapy**: Work with a counselor or therapist to process deep-seated pain and trauma.
5. **Service to Others**: Transform pain into purpose by helping others who face similar challenges.

Stories of Transformation: Learning from Pain

Pain is a recurring theme in myths, literature, and real-life stories, often serving as the catalyst for transformation. Consider these examples:

1. **The Phoenix**: In mythology, the phoenix rises from the ashes of its own destruction, symbolizing the renewal that emerges from pain.
2. **Viktor Frankl**: In his book *Man's Search for Meaning*, Frankl describes finding purpose and hope even in the suffering of a concentration camp.
3. **Your Own Story**: Reflect on moments in your life when pain led to growth, new perspectives, or unexpected opportunities.

The Rewards of Transforming Pain
When you transform pain into wisdom, you gain:

1. **Resilience**: The ability to navigate future challenges with courage and confidence.
2. **Self-Awareness**: A deeper understanding of your emotions, values, and needs.
3. **Empathy**: Greater compassion for others who experience pain.
4. **Empowerment**: The realization that pain does not define you—it empowers you.

Moving Forward: Embracing the Wisdom of Pain
Pain is not something to fear or avoid; it is a profound teacher that guides us toward greater understanding and growth. By engaging with your pain and transforming it into wisdom, you embrace the fullness of your humanity and unlock your potential for resilience, compassion, and self-awareness.

Chapter 10: Embracing the Unknown: Lessons from Chaos and Mystery

Life is filled with uncertainty, unpredictability, and moments of chaos. While these experiences can be unsettling, they are also fertile ground for growth, creativity, and transformation. Embracing the unknown requires courage and a willingness to surrender control, allowing us to navigate the mysteries of existence with curiosity and grace. This chapter explores how chaos and mystery can be powerful teachers, offering lessons that help us expand our understanding of ourselves and the world.

By delving into the nature of the unknown, we'll examine its role in personal development, uncover techniques to engage with it constructively, and learn to find meaning in its challenges. Through this journey, you will discover how embracing chaos and mystery can lead to profound insight and empowerment.

The Nature of the Unknown: Chaos and Mystery Defined

The unknown represents all that lies beyond the boundaries of our current understanding. It is the uncharted territory of our lives—future possibilities, unexplored aspects of ourselves, and the mysteries of the universe. Chaos, on the other hand, refers to the disorder and unpredictability that often accompany the unknown.

Characteristics of the Unknown:

1. **Unpredictability**: The unknown defies certainty and linear planning.
2. **Ambiguity**: It is neither inherently good nor bad, simply undefined.
3. **Potential**: Within the unknown lies infinite possibility for creation and transformation.

Characteristics of Chaos:

1. **Disruption**: Chaos upends routines, expectations, and assumptions.
2. **Creativity**: Disorder often precedes innovation and growth.
3. **Tension**: Chaos can evoke fear but also energize exploration.

The Role of Chaos and Mystery in Personal Growth

Chaos and mystery are integral to personal development, challenging us to step outside our comfort zones and expand our perspectives. They often appear during major life transitions, crises, or moments of profound introspection.

Key Lessons from Chaos and Mystery:

1. **Adaptability**: Chaos teaches us to remain flexible and open-minded in the face of uncertainty.
2. **Resilience**: Facing the unknown builds emotional strength and confidence in navigating life's challenges.
3. **Creativity**: Mystery sparks curiosity and inspires new ways of thinking.
4. **Self-Discovery**: Engaging with the unknown reveals hidden aspects of our identity and potential.

Why We Fear the Unknown

The unknown is often accompanied by fear, as it challenges our need for security, control, and predictability. Understanding this fear is the first step toward overcoming it.

Common Fears Associated with the Unknown:

1. **Fear of Failure**: Worrying about making mistakes or encountering setbacks in unfamiliar situations.
2. **Fear of Vulnerability**: The discomfort of feeling exposed or unprepared.
3. **Fear of Change**: Resistance to letting go of the familiar, even when it no longer serves us.
4. **Fear of the Shadow**: The unknown often mirrors our own unexplored depths, bringing hidden fears and insecurities to light.

Reframing the Unknown: From Threat to Opportunity

Reframing the unknown as an opportunity rather than a threat is a transformative shift in perspective. Instead of resisting chaos and mystery, we can learn to embrace them as catalysts for growth and discovery.

Reframing Questions:

- What might I learn from this experience?
- How can this uncertainty inspire creativity or innovation?
- What opportunities might emerge from this chaos?
- How can embracing the unknown strengthen my resilience?

Tools and Techniques for Embracing the Unknown

Engaging with chaos and mystery requires a combination of mindset shifts and practical strategies. The following tools can help you navigate the unknown with confidence and curiosity:

1. Cultivate a Beginner's Mind

The concept of "beginner's mind" comes from Zen Buddhism and involves approaching every experience with openness and curiosity, free from preconceived notions or judgments.

Practice:

- Imagine encountering a situation as if for the first time.
- Ask questions like: "What can I learn from this?" or "What possibilities exist here that I haven't considered?"
- Release the need for immediate answers or certainty.

2. Develop Emotional Resilience

Resilience helps you maintain stability and confidence amid chaos. Building resilience involves managing stress, embracing discomfort, and staying grounded.

Techniques:

- **Mindfulness Meditation**: Focus on the present moment to reduce anxiety about the future.
- **Gratitude Practice**: Reflect on what remains constant and supportive in your life.
- **Affirmations**: Use empowering statements like "I can handle whatever comes my way" or "Uncertainty is a gateway to growth."

3. Lean into Uncertainty

Instead of avoiding uncertainty, practice stepping into it deliberately. This can help desensitize you to fear and build confidence in navigating the unknown.

Exercises:

- Try something new, such as a hobby, activity, or experience that pushes you out of your comfort zone.
- Make small decisions without overanalyzing outcomes, trusting your instincts.
- Embrace "not knowing" as an integral part of discovery.

4. Engage with Mystery

Mystery can be a source of wonder and inspiration. Engage with the unknown by exploring it through creative and reflective practices.

Ideas:

- **Storytelling**: Write or imagine stories about possibilities within the unknown.
- **Artistic Expression**: Paint, draw, or create without a predetermined outcome, allowing the process to unfold organically.
- **Symbolism**: Work with symbols, myths, or archetypes that resonate with the themes of chaos and mystery.

5. Seek Balance Between Order and Chaos

While chaos fosters growth, too much disorder can be overwhelming. Balance the exploration of the unknown with structures that provide stability.

Strategies:

- Establish daily routines to anchor yourself during periods of uncertainty.
- Create a safe space (physically or emotionally) where you can retreat and recharge.
- Set small, achievable goals to maintain a sense of progress.

6. Learn from Nature

Nature offers powerful metaphors for navigating chaos and mystery. The cycles of growth, decay, and renewal remind us that change and uncertainty are natural processes.

Reflection Exercise:

- Spend time in nature observing patterns of chaos and order, such as waves, weather, or animal behavior.
- Reflect on how these patterns mirror your own experiences of the unknown.

The Wisdom of Myths and Stories About Chaos

Throughout history, myths and stories have explored the interplay between chaos and order, providing timeless insights into navigating the unknown. Consider the following examples:

1. **Pandora's Box**: Although opening the box unleashed chaos, it also revealed hope—reminding us that even in uncertainty, there is potential for renewal.
2. **The Hero's Journey**: Every hero must venture into the unknown, confronting chaos to discover inner strength and wisdom.
3. **The Taoist Perspective**: In Taoism, chaos is seen as a precursor to harmony, symbolized by the dynamic balance of yin and yang.

These stories teach us that chaos and mystery are not adversaries but essential elements of transformation.

Transforming Chaos into Growth

Embracing chaos and mystery allows us to access untapped potential and discover new dimensions of ourselves. Transformation begins with a mindset of openness and a willingness to step into the unknown.

Steps to Transform Chaos:

1. Recognize the opportunity within disruption.
2. Identify what you can control and release what you cannot.
3. Focus on the present moment, letting go of anxiety about the future.
4. Trust in your ability to adapt and learn.

Moving Forward: Living with Mystery

Living with mystery means accepting that not all questions have answers and not all paths are clear. It is a practice of surrendering control and finding beauty in the unknown. By embracing chaos and mystery, you cultivate a deeper connection to yourself, others, and the world.

As you continue your journey, remember that the unknown is not something to conquer—it is something to explore. Each step into the mysterious expands your understanding and strengthens your capacity for growth. In the next chapter, we will explore how to integrate the lessons of the unknown into your daily life, creating a harmonious balance between exploration and stability. For now, embrace the chaos, honor the mystery, and trust in the unfolding of your path.

Part 3: Crafting Your Personal Myth

Chapter 11: The Power of Storytelling: Weaving Narrative Threads

Storytelling is one of humanity's oldest and most profound tools for making sense of the world. Through stories, we convey knowledge, express emotions, and connect to one another. But storytelling is more than a way to entertain or inform; it is also a powerful means of personal transformation. The narratives we create about ourselves shape our identity, influence our choices, and determine how we experience life.

In this chapter, we explore the transformative power of storytelling, examining how personal narratives shape reality, how to rewrite disempowering stories, and how to weave narrative threads that align with your authentic self. By mastering the art of storytelling, you can harness its power to heal, grow, and connect deeply with yourself and others.

The Human Connection to Storytelling

Storytelling is universal. Across cultures and time periods, humans have relied on stories to share experiences, preserve history, and explain the mysteries of existence. The power of storytelling lies in its ability to resonate emotionally and communicate complex ideas in relatable ways.

Why Stories Matter:

1. **Meaning-Making**: Stories help us make sense of chaos, offering structure and coherence to our experiences.
2. **Emotional Connection**: Stories evoke empathy and shared understanding, bridging gaps between individuals and communities.
3. **Memory Enhancement**: Narratives engage the brain more effectively than isolated facts, making them memorable and impactful.

In essence, storytelling is the lens through which we view and interpret reality, giving shape to our inner and outer worlds.

Personal Narratives: The Stories We Tell Ourselves

The most powerful stories are not the ones we read in books or watch in movies—they are the ones we tell ourselves. These personal narratives form the foundation of our identity, shaping how we see ourselves and how we interact with the world.

Key Elements of Personal Narratives:

1. **Identity**: Who we believe we are.
2. **Beliefs**: What we consider true about ourselves, others, and life.
3. **Values**: What we prioritize and strive for.
4. **Goals**: What we aim to achieve based on our narrative.

Example:

A person who views themselves as a "survivor" might approach challenges with resilience, while someone who sees themselves as a "failure" may struggle to take risks or embrace opportunities.

The Shadow in Personal Narratives

The shadow plays a significant role in shaping personal narratives. Unacknowledged fears, desires, and insecurities often influence the stories we create, leading to limiting beliefs or self-sabotaging patterns.

Common Shadow Narratives:

- "I'm not good enough."
- "People will always hurt me."
- "I can't succeed no matter how hard I try."

These narratives can feel inescapable, but they are not absolute truths. By identifying and confronting the shadow's influence, you can rewrite these stories to reflect your authentic self.

The Science of Storytelling and the Brain

Neuroscience reveals that storytelling engages multiple regions of the brain, making it a powerful tool for change. When we hear or create a story, our brain releases chemicals like **oxytocin**, which fosters empathy and trust, and **dopamine**, which enhances focus and memory. This biological response underscores storytelling's potential to reshape our thoughts and behaviors.

Neuroplasticity and Storytelling:

The brain's ability to rewire itself—known as neuroplasticity—allows us to rewrite personal narratives. By intentionally crafting empowering stories, we can replace limiting beliefs with new patterns of thought and action.

Rewriting Disempowering Stories: A Step-by-Step Guide

Rewriting your personal narrative is an act of self-empowerment. It involves identifying stories that no longer serve you, reframing them, and creating new ones that align with your values and aspirations.

Step 1: Identify Your Current Narrative

Reflect on the stories you tell yourself about who you are, what you're capable of, and how the world works. These narratives often emerge in moments of self-doubt, decision-making, or conflict.

Exercise:

Write down the following:

- A story you tell yourself about your identity (e.g., "I'm not creative" or "I always mess things up").
- A recurring belief about your abilities or worth.
- Patterns in your relationships or career that reflect your narrative.

Step 2: Analyze the Origins of Your Narrative

Understanding where your story comes from can help you see it as a construct rather than an absolute truth. Consider:

- **Childhood Experiences**: Did a parent, teacher, or peer reinforce this story?
- **Societal Influences**: Does this narrative align with cultural expectations or stereotypes?
- **Trauma or Failure**: Was this story born from a specific painful experience?

Example:

If you believe "I'm not good enough," it might stem from a childhood where praise was rare, or mistakes were harshly criticized.

Step 3: Challenge and Reframe the Narrative

Disempowering stories often rest on faulty assumptions or outdated beliefs. Challenge these narratives by questioning their validity and reframing them in a way that reflects your growth and potential.

Questions to Challenge Your Narrative:

- Is this story objectively true?
- What evidence contradicts this belief?
- How would I rewrite this story if I were my best friend?

Reframing Example:

Old Narrative: "I always fail at everything I try."

Reframed Narrative: "Every failure has taught me valuable lessons and brought me closer to success."

Step 4: Craft a New Empowering Narrative

Create a story that aligns with your values, strengths, and aspirations. This new narrative should inspire and motivate you, serving as a guiding thread in your life.

Tips for Crafting Your Narrative:

- **Use Positive Language**: Focus on growth, possibility, and resilience.
- **Include Challenges**: Acknowledge past struggles as stepping stones to where you are now.
- **Anchor in Authenticity**: Ensure the story feels true to your experiences and aspirations.

Example:

New Narrative: "I am resilient and resourceful. Every challenge I face is an opportunity to grow and create a better version of myself."

Weaving Narrative Threads into Daily Life

A new narrative is only powerful if it is integrated into your daily life. Practice living your story through intentional actions and affirmations.

Practical Steps:

1. **Daily Affirmations**: Repeat phrases from your new narrative to reinforce its truth.
2. **Mindful Decisions**: Make choices aligned with your empowering story.
3. **Visualization**: Imagine yourself embodying the traits and values of your narrative in real-life scenarios.
4. **Celebrate Progress**: Acknowledge small wins that reflect your new story.

The Collective Power of Storytelling

While personal narratives are deeply individual, storytelling also connects us to the collective human experience. Sharing your story can:

- Foster empathy and understanding in others.
- Inspire those facing similar challenges.
- Deepen connections within your community.

Exercise:

Share a story about a pivotal moment in your life with someone you trust or through a creative medium, such as writing or art. Reflect on how sharing your story affects both you and your audience.

Myths, Archetypes, and Universal Stories

The narratives we craft often mirror universal myths and archetypes. Recognizing these patterns can help you understand your role in the larger story of life.

Common Archetypes in Personal Narratives:

- **The Hero**: Overcomes adversity to achieve growth and transformation.
- **The Rebel**: Challenges norms to forge a unique path.
- **The Healer**: Turns pain into wisdom to aid others.

Reflection:

Which archetype resonates with your current narrative? How might it evolve in your next chapter?

The Transformative Power of Owning Your Story

Owning your story means taking responsibility for the narrative you live by. It is an act of empowerment that allows you to shape your destiny rather than be defined by circumstances.

Key Takeaways:

- Your story is a dynamic, evolving creation—not a fixed reality.
- Every experience, even painful ones, can contribute to a meaningful narrative.
- By rewriting your story, you reclaim agency over your life and inspire others to do the same.

Moving Forward: Becoming the Author of Your Life

Storytelling is both an art and a practice. As you refine your narrative, remember that you are the author of your life. Each moment offers an opportunity to weave new threads, explore untold possibilities, and align your story with your truest self.

Chapter 12: Archetypes Within: Identifying Your Mythic Roles

Archetypes are universal symbols and patterns of behavior that exist in the collective unconscious, a concept introduced by Carl Jung. These archetypes shape our thoughts, emotions, and actions, influencing how we perceive ourselves and the roles we play in life. By identifying and understanding your inner archetypes, you gain insight into your motivations, strengths, and challenges. This awareness allows you to harness their power for personal growth and self-discovery.

In this chapter, we will explore the concept of archetypes, their significance in personal mythology, and how to identify the mythic roles that resonate with your life journey. By engaging with your archetypes, you can uncover hidden aspects of yourself, integrate your shadow, and live more authentically.

What Are Archetypes?

Archetypes are universal patterns or roles that appear across cultures, myths, and stories. They represent fundamental aspects of human experience, such as the hero's quest for meaning, the caregiver's nurturing instinct, or the rebel's desire for change. While these archetypes are collective in nature, they manifest uniquely within each individual.

Key Features of Archetypes:

1. **Universal**: Found across cultures and time periods, archetypes transcend individual experiences.
2. **Symbolic**: Represent fundamental human drives, fears, and desires.
3. **Dynamic**: Archetypes evolve and interact, reflecting the complexity of human nature.
4. **Personal**: Each person embodies archetypes in ways that align with their unique experiences and personality.

The Role of Archetypes in Personal Growth

Archetypes act as mirrors, reflecting different facets of your personality and behavior. By identifying your archetypes, you can gain a deeper understanding of your internal world and how it shapes your interactions with the external world.

Why Explore Your Archetypes?

- **Self-Awareness**: Discover hidden aspects of your personality and motivations.
- **Integration**: Balance and integrate conflicting parts of yourself.
- **Empowerment**: Recognize and embrace your strengths and potential.
- **Healing**: Address wounds or challenges associated with specific archetypes.
- **Purpose**: Align with archetypal roles that resonate with your life's mission.

Common Archetypes and Their Characteristics

While there are countless archetypes, some are particularly prominent in myths, literature, and personal development. Below are a few key archetypes, along with their traits, strengths, and shadow aspects:

1. The Hero

- **Traits**: Courage, determination, ambition.
- **Strengths**: Overcomes challenges, inspires others, seeks growth.
- **Shadow**: Arrogance, fear of failure, excessive self-reliance.

The Hero represents the part of you that seeks to overcome obstacles and achieve greatness. The shadow of the Hero emerges when the pursuit of success leads to burnout or isolation.

2. The Caregiver

- **Traits**: Compassion, generosity, nurturing.
- **Strengths**: Provides support and healing, fosters community.
- **Shadow**: Over-sacrifice, enabling, neglecting personal needs.

The Caregiver reflects your instinct to nurture and protect others. Its shadow appears when you neglect your own well-being in favor of others.

3. The Rebel

- **Traits**: Independence, defiance, innovation.
- **Strengths**: Challenges norms, drives change, advocates for justice.
- **Shadow**: Destructiveness, impulsivity, alienation.

The Rebel represents your desire to break free from constraints and forge new paths. Its shadow manifests as chaos or reckless behavior.

4. The Sage

- **Traits**: Wisdom, knowledge, insight.
- **Strengths**: Seeks truth, mentors others, provides clarity.
- **Shadow**: Arrogance, detachment, intellectual superiority.

The Sage embodies your quest for understanding and the pursuit of deeper meaning. Its shadow emerges when knowledge becomes a tool for judgment or control.

5. The Lover

- **Traits**: Passion, connection, intimacy.
- **Strengths**: Fosters relationships, inspires creativity, embraces joy.
- **Shadow**: Dependency, jealousy, fear of loss.

The Lover reflects your capacity for deep emotional connections and appreciation of beauty. Its shadow appears when love becomes possessive or overwhelming.

6. The Magician

- **Traits**: Creativity, transformation, vision.
- **Strengths**: Transforms situations, manifests goals, inspires wonder.
- **Shadow**: Manipulation, deceit, overreliance on control.

The Magician represents your ability to create change and see possibilities beyond the ordinary. Its shadow manifests as a misuse of power or fear of failure.

7. The Explorer

- **Traits**: Curiosity, adventure, freedom.
- **Strengths**: Seeks new experiences, expands horizons, embraces change.
- **Shadow**: Restlessness, aimlessness, fear of commitment.

The Explorer reflects your desire for discovery and personal growth. Its shadow emerges when exploration becomes avoidance or dissatisfaction.

8. The Ruler

- **Traits**: Leadership, authority, responsibility.
- **Strengths**: Creates stability, protects others, establishes order.
- **Shadow**: Tyranny, control, fear of vulnerability.

The Ruler represents your ability to take charge and create structure. Its shadow appears when power becomes oppressive or inflexible.

Identifying Your Archetypes: A Practical Guide

To identify your archetypes, reflect on your behaviors, values, and life patterns. Consider the roles you naturally embody, the traits you admire or dislike in others, and the recurring themes in your life story.

Step 1: Reflect on Your Life Story

Your life experiences often reveal the archetypes that are most active within you. Look for patterns, key moments, and roles you've played in relationships, careers, or challenges.

Exercise:

Write down significant events or turning points in your life. For each, consider:

- What role did I play in this situation?
- What strengths or traits emerged?
- What challenges or shadows did I face?

Step 2: Observe Your Patterns and Behaviors

Pay attention to recurring patterns in your thoughts, actions, and emotions. These can provide clues about dominant archetypes.

Questions for Reflection:

- What motivates me most?
- What roles do I naturally take on in groups or relationships?
- What traits do I admire or aspire to embody?
- What traits in others provoke strong reactions in me (positive or negative)?

Step 3: Engage with Archetypal Symbols and Stories

Archetypes are often expressed through myths, literature, and art. Explore stories, characters, or symbols that resonate with you to uncover your archetypes.

Exercise:

List your favorite books, movies, or myths. Identify characters or themes that feel personally significant. Consider how they mirror aspects of your personality or aspirations.

Step 4: Use Archetype Assessment Tools

Several tools and frameworks can help identify your archetypes, including:

- **The Jungian Archetype Test:** Online assessments based on Jung's theories.
- **The Heroine's Journey or Hero's Journey Framework:** Reflecting on your life through mythic stages.
- **Tarot or Symbolic Tools:** Using symbolic imagery to explore unconscious archetypes.

Step 5: Reflect on Your Shadows

Each archetype has a shadow side that reveals challenges and areas for growth. Reflect on how these shadows manifest in your life and how they might point to unresolved issues or unmet needs.

Exercise:

For each archetype you identify, ask:

- How does this archetype serve me?
- How does its shadow limit me?
- How can I integrate its lessons into my life?

Integrating Archetypes into Daily Life

Once you've identified your archetypes, the next step is to integrate them into your life. This involves embracing their strengths, addressing their shadows, and using them as tools for growth and self-expression.

Practical Tips:

1. **Embrace Strengths**: Acknowledge and celebrate the gifts each archetype brings to your life.
2. **Balance Shadows**: Work on integrating the shadow aspects of your archetypes, turning challenges into opportunities for growth.
3. **Activate Dormant Archetypes**: Explore archetypes you feel disconnected from to expand your sense of self.
4. **Use Archetypes for Decision-Making**: Reflect on which archetype's perspective would best guide you in a given situation.

Living Your Mythic Roles

Identifying and embracing your archetypes allows you to live more intentionally, aligning your actions with your authentic self. As you navigate life's challenges and opportunities, your archetypes serve as allies and guides, helping you create a meaningful and fulfilling narrative.

Reflection Questions:

- How can I embody my archetypes more fully in my daily life?
- What archetype do I want to activate or develop further?
- How do my archetypes support my personal growth and life purpose?

Moving Forward: The Power of Archetypal Awareness

Your archetypes are dynamic, evolving aspects of your inner world. By engaging with them consciously, you can unlock their transformative power, deepening your self-awareness and enhancing your capacity for growth. In the next chapter, we will explore how to integrate the lessons of your archetypes with the broader themes of shadow work, storytelling, and personal transformation, weaving them into a cohesive and empowered sense of self. For now, honor the mythic roles you embody and trust in their wisdom to guide your journey.

Chapter 13: Symbols and Motifs: Creating a Unique Mythic Language

Symbols and motifs are the building blocks of mythology, art, and personal narratives. They serve as powerful tools for expressing abstract ideas, emotions, and themes, offering a language that transcends words. By creating a unique mythic language through symbols and motifs, you can deepen your understanding of yourself and your journey, forge a connection to your subconscious, and craft a personal mythology that resonates with your inner truth.

This chapter explores the role of symbols and motifs in mythology, psychology, and storytelling. We'll examine how to identify and create symbols that reflect your experiences and values, how motifs can bring coherence to your personal narrative, and how to use your mythic language as a tool for self-discovery and transformation.

Understanding Symbols and Motifs

What Are Symbols?

Symbols are images, objects, or concepts that represent larger ideas or themes. They are deeply personal yet universally resonant, connecting individual experiences to collective archetypes.

Examples of Symbols:

- **The Sun**: Represents life, vitality, and enlightenment.
- **The Tree**: Symbolizes growth, connection, and rootedness.
- **The Labyrinth**: Reflects complexity, mystery, and self-discovery.

What Are Motifs?

Motifs are recurring themes, patterns, or elements that appear consistently in a narrative or artistic expression. They provide structure and unity to stories, guiding the audience toward deeper meaning.

Examples of Motifs:

- **Journeys**: Physical or emotional quests symbolize transformation.
- **Light and Darkness**: Represents duality, morality, and insight.
- **Cycles**: Recurring patterns like seasons or life stages reflect renewal and inevitability.

Together, symbols and motifs create a visual and conceptual language that enriches storytelling, self-expression, and introspection.

The Role of Symbols and Motifs in Myth and Psychology

Symbols and motifs are integral to both mythology and psychology, serving as bridges between the conscious and unconscious mind.

In Mythology:

- **Symbolic Imagery**: Myths often use symbols to represent universal truths. For example, the phoenix represents rebirth and resilience, while the serpent symbolizes transformation and hidden knowledge.
- **Motif Repetition**: Recurring motifs like the hero's journey, the descent into the underworld, or the cosmic tree unify myths across cultures.

In Psychology:

- **Jungian Symbols**: Carl Jung viewed symbols as expressions of the collective unconscious. He believed that symbols like mandalas and archetypes help individuals navigate their inner worlds.
- **Dream Analysis**: Symbols in dreams reveal unconscious thoughts, desires, and fears, offering insight into the psyche.

By incorporating symbols and motifs into your personal mythology, you can tap into their transformative potential, using them to explore your shadow, express your aspirations, and understand your life's narrative.

Identifying Personal Symbols and Motifs

To create a unique mythic language, begin by identifying the symbols and motifs that resonate most deeply with you. These may be drawn from your personal experiences, cultural influences, or intuitive insights.

Step 1: Reflect on Personal Experiences

Symbols often emerge from significant moments in your life. Reflect on events, emotions, and memories that have shaped you.

Exercise:

- List five pivotal experiences in your life (e.g., a triumph, a loss, a transformative journey).
- For each, identify an object, image, or concept that represents the experience.

Example:

- Pivotal experience: Moving to a new city.
- Symbol: A compass, representing navigation and finding direction.

Step 2: Explore Cultural and Universal Symbols

While personal symbols are unique to your story, cultural and universal symbols connect you to broader human experiences. Consider symbols that appear in art, literature, or spiritual traditions that resonate with you.

Exercise:

- Research symbols from different cultures and mythologies.
- Note which ones evoke a strong emotional or intuitive response.

Example:

The lotus, a symbol of enlightenment and resilience in Eastern traditions, may resonate with your journey of overcoming adversity.

Step 3: Pay Attention to Dreams and Intuition

Dreams and intuition often reveal symbols that are deeply connected to your subconscious.

Exercise:

- Keep a dream journal. Write down recurring images, characters, or settings.
- Meditate or visualize to allow symbols to arise spontaneously.

Example:

A recurring dream of flying might suggest freedom or a desire to rise above challenges.

Step 4: Identify Recurring Motifs in Your Life

Look for patterns or recurring themes in your experiences, values, and aspirations. These motifs provide coherence and depth to your personal mythology.

Questions for Reflection:

- What themes or patterns consistently appear in my life?
- What lessons or challenges seem to repeat?
- What values or ideals guide my decisions?

Example:

A recurring motif of water might reflect emotional depth, renewal, or the flow of life.

Creating Your Mythic Language

Once you've identified your symbols and motifs, weave them into a cohesive mythic language that reflects your unique narrative. This process involves defining the meaning of each symbol, organizing motifs into a structure, and using them intentionally in your life.

Step 1: Define the Meaning of Your Symbols

Give each symbol a clear and personal meaning. This helps anchor it in your story while allowing it to evolve over time.

Exercise: Create a symbolic dictionary. For each symbol, write:

- Its visual representation.
- Its meaning in your personal mythology.
- Its emotional or thematic significance.

Example:

- **Symbol**: The Moon.
- **Meaning**: Intuition, reflection, and hidden potential.
- **Significance**: Represents my connection to inner wisdom and the unknown.

Step 2: Organize Your Motifs

Motifs create structure and continuity in your mythic language. Organize them into categories or themes that reflect different aspects of your life.

Examples of Motif Categories:

- **Transformation**: Symbols and patterns related to growth and change (e.g., the butterfly, fire).
- **Connection**: Representations of relationships and community (e.g., the tree, the circle).
- **Resilience**: Themes of strength and endurance (e.g., the mountain, the phoenix).

Step 3: Use Symbols and Motifs Intentionally

Incorporate your mythic language into your daily life, creative expressions, and personal growth practices.

Ways to Use Your Mythic Language:

1. **Art and Writing**: Use your symbols and motifs in journaling, storytelling, or visual art to express your inner world.
2. **Rituals and Practices**: Create rituals that incorporate your symbols, such as lighting a candle to honor transformation or wearing jewelry with symbolic meaning.
3. **Decision-Making**: Reflect on your motifs when facing choices or challenges. For example, ask yourself, "What would the mountain (resilience) guide me to do in this situation?"
4. **Dream Work**: Use your symbolic dictionary to analyze dreams and explore their connection to your personal mythology.

The Evolving Nature of Symbols

Symbols and motifs are not static; they evolve as you grow and change. A symbol that once represented fear may later come to signify courage, reflecting your journey of transformation.

Example:

The labyrinth might initially symbolize confusion and being lost but later transform into a representation of discovery and self-mastery.

Connecting Your Mythic Language to the Collective

While your mythic language is deeply personal, it also connects you to the universal human experience. Sharing your symbols and motifs can foster empathy, inspire others, and strengthen your connection to a larger narrative.

Exercise:

- Create a visual or written representation of your mythic language (e.g., a mandala, a story, or a symbolic map).
- Share it with trusted friends, a creative community, or a spiritual group to explore its resonance with others.

Moving Forward: Living Your Mythic Language

Your symbols and motifs are powerful tools for self-expression, introspection, and growth. As you continue your journey, let your mythic language guide you in creating a life that reflects your authentic self.

Reflection Questions:

- How can I honor my symbols and motifs in my daily life?
- What new symbols or motifs might emerge as I continue to grow?
- How can my mythic language inspire or support others?

Chapter 14: Building Your Mythic World: Setting the Stage

A mythic world is a personal and symbolic space where your inner truths, archetypes, and narratives come to life. It acts as a mirror of your inner self, a sanctuary for reflection, and a canvas for creativity. Building your mythic world allows you to externalize the themes, symbols, and motifs of your personal mythology, giving them structure and coherence. By setting the stage for this world, you deepen your connection to your inner journey and empower yourself to navigate life with clarity and purpose.

In this chapter, we'll explore the concept of a mythic world, why it's valuable, and how to create one that reflects your unique identity and aspirations. Through step-by-step guidance, you'll learn to construct a symbolic landscape, populate it with meaningful elements, and use it as a tool for self-discovery and transformation.

What Is a Mythic World?

A mythic world is a symbolic, imaginative realm where your personal mythology unfolds. It is both a reflection of your inner psyche and a creative expression of your values, desires, and challenges. This world can be visualized, written, drawn, or even acted out, serving as a living framework for your growth and exploration.

Characteristics of a Mythic World:

1. **Symbolic**: Every element—landscapes, characters, objects—represents an aspect of your inner life or journey.
2. **Dynamic**: It evolves as you grow, adapt, and integrate new experiences.
3. **Personal**: While inspired by universal archetypes and motifs, your mythic world is unique to you.
4. **Sacred**: It is a space for introspection, healing, and transformation.

The Value of Building a Mythic World

Creating a mythic world offers more than creative expression—it becomes a powerful tool for self-understanding, problem-solving, and personal growth.

Why Build a Mythic World?

1. **Self-Reflection**: Externalizing your inner world helps you identify patterns, desires, and challenges.
2. **Emotional Processing**: Symbolic representation allows you to explore and resolve emotions safely.
3. **Empowerment**: Your mythic world is a realm where you are the creator, instilling a sense of agency.
4. **Integration**: It provides a space to unite your archetypes, symbols, and narratives into a cohesive whole.
5. **Inspiration**: Engaging with your mythic world sparks creativity and imagination.

Step-by-Step Guide to Building Your Mythic World

Building your mythic world is a deeply personal process that unfolds over time. Below is a comprehensive guide to help you set the stage and bring your world to life.

Step 1: Define the Purpose of Your Mythic World

Before you begin, reflect on what you hope to achieve or explore through your mythic world.

Questions for Reflection:

- What aspects of myself or my life do I want to understand better?
- How can my mythic world support my personal growth or healing?
- What emotions, themes, or experiences do I want to explore?

Example:

Your mythic world might serve as a space for self-discovery, helping you navigate transitions or confront fears.

Step 2: Choose a Form for Your World

Your mythic world can take many forms, depending on your preferences and creative style.

Examples of Forms:

- **Visual**: A map, painting, or collage.
- **Written**: A journal, story, or detailed descriptions of landscapes and characters.
- **Interactive**: A ritual space, role-playing game, or guided visualization.
- **Mixed Media**: A combination of visual, written, and physical elements.

Step 3: Create the Landscape

The landscape of your mythic world reflects your inner psyche and serves as the stage for your personal mythology. Consider the symbolic significance of its elements.

Key Elements of the Landscape:

1. **Geography**: Mountains, forests, oceans, deserts—each terrain symbolizes different aspects of your inner journey.
    - **Mountains**: Challenges, growth, and perspective.
    - **Forests**: Mystery, intuition, and transformation.
    - **Oceans**: Depth, emotions, and the subconscious.
    - **Deserts**: Isolation, resilience, and clarity.
2. **Boundaries**: Define the edges of your world, whether they are physical (walls, oceans) or conceptual (a liminal space between reality and imagination).
3. **Sacred Spaces**: Include areas for reflection or ritual, such as temples, altars, or sanctuaries.

Exercise: Draw or describe your mythic landscape. Include at least three distinct terrains or locations and reflect on their meanings.

Step 4: Populate Your World with Symbols

Symbols are the lifeblood of your mythic world. Populate your landscape with objects, creatures, or features that hold personal meaning.

Examples of Symbols:

- **Objects**: A key (unlocking potential), a mirror (self-reflection), a lantern (guidance).
- **Creatures**: A phoenix (rebirth), a serpent (transformation), a wolf (intuition).
- **Structures**: A tower (aspiration), a bridge (connection), a labyrinth (self-discovery).

Exercise:

- Identify five symbols that resonate with your personal mythology.
- Place them within your mythic world, considering their significance and interactions with the environment.

Step 5: Introduce Archetypes and Characters

Archetypes and characters represent facets of your personality, shadow, and aspirations. They are the actors in your mythic narrative.

Key Questions:

- Which archetypes are most active in my life right now?
- What new archetypes or characters do I want to explore?
- How do these figures interact with one another?

Examples:

- **The Hero**: Embarks on quests and overcomes challenges.
- **The Sage**: Offers wisdom and insight.
- **The Shadow**: Represents fears and hidden desires.

Exercise: Write a short profile for each archetype or character in your world. Include their traits, strengths, shadows, and role in your mythic narrative.

Step 6: Establish Themes and Motifs

Themes and motifs give your mythic world cohesion and depth, reflecting your personal journey.

Examples of Themes:

- Transformation and rebirth.
- Light and shadow.
- Connection and isolation.

Exercise: Choose 2-3 central themes for your mythic world. Reflect on how they influence the landscape, symbols, and characters.

Step 7: Engage with Your World

Your mythic world is not a static creation—it is a living, evolving space that you interact with regularly.

Ways to Engage:

1. **Meditation and Visualization**: Imagine yourself walking through your mythic world, observing its elements and interacting with its characters.
2. **Storytelling**: Write or narrate stories that take place in your world, exploring its dynamics and lessons.
3. **Art and Ritual**: Create artwork or rituals inspired by your mythic world to deepen your connection.
4. **Problem-Solving**: Use your world as a symbolic space to explore challenges and possibilities in your real life.

Evolving Your Mythic World

As you grow, your mythic world will evolve to reflect new insights, challenges, and aspirations. Embrace this evolution as part of the creative process.

Questions for Reflection:

- What changes have occurred in my mythic world recently?
- How do these changes mirror shifts in my life or mindset?
- What new elements or themes might I introduce?

Examples of Mythic Worlds

To inspire your process, here are examples of mythic worlds and their symbolic significance:

1. **The Garden of Renewal**: A lush, ever-changing garden representing healing and growth.
2. **The Island of Solitude**: A remote island reflecting introspection and self-discovery.
3. **The Realm of Shadows**: A mysterious, twilight world where fears are confronted and integrated.
4. **The City of Light**: A vibrant, interconnected metropolis symbolizing connection and creativity.

Moving Forward: Living in Your Mythic World

Your mythic world is not just a creative exercise—it is a tool for transformation and empowerment. By regularly engaging with this space, you can explore your inner depths, express your unique mythology, and navigate life with intention and clarity.

Reflection Questions:

- How can I use my mythic world to address current challenges or goals?
- What lessons or insights has my world revealed?
- How can I share the inspiration of my mythic world with others?

Chapter 15: Writing the Myth: Crafting the First Chapter of Your Journey

Every myth begins with a call to adventure, a moment when the protagonist steps onto the path of transformation. In your personal mythology, the first chapter serves as the foundation of your journey. It sets the tone, introduces your symbolic world, and defines the themes and challenges that will shape your growth. Writing this chapter is both an act of creativity and self-discovery, as it requires you to weave together your archetypes, symbols, and motifs into a cohesive narrative.

This chapter provides a comprehensive guide to crafting the first chapter of your mythic journey. You will explore the elements of mythic storytelling, develop a compelling opening, and learn to incorporate your personal symbols and archetypes into your narrative. By the end, you'll have a tangible expression of your mythic self and the confidence to continue writing your story.

The Purpose of the First Chapter

The first chapter of your myth is more than an introduction—it is an invitation to step into your story with intention and awareness. It establishes the foundation for your journey by defining key elements and setting the stage for transformation.

Key Goals of the First Chapter:

1. **Set the Scene**: Introduce the symbolic world where your journey unfolds.
2. **Define the Protagonist**: Establish your mythic role and its connection to your personal identity.
3. **Present the Call to Adventure**: Highlight the event or realization that sparks your journey.
4. **Introduce Conflict or Challenge**: Identify the initial obstacle or shadow element that you must confront.
5. **Establish Themes**: Lay the groundwork for the recurring motifs and lessons of your story.

Elements of a Mythic First Chapter

To craft a compelling first chapter, you must integrate key storytelling elements that resonate with your personal mythology.

1. The Protagonist: You as the Hero

The protagonist is the central figure in your myth. While this character is a symbolic version of yourself, it reflects your inner truths, aspirations, and challenges.

Questions to Define Your Protagonist:

- What archetype(s) does my protagonist embody?
- What qualities or traits define their character?
- What fears, flaws, or shadows must they confront?
- What motivates them to begin this journey?

Example:

A protagonist might embody the Explorer archetype, driven by curiosity and a longing for freedom, but struggling with a fear of failure.

2. The Setting: Your Symbolic World

The setting provides the backdrop for your mythic journey, reflecting the themes and challenges you face in your life.

Key Considerations for the Setting:

- How does the landscape reflect the protagonist's inner state?
- What symbols and motifs define the environment?
- Is the world in balance, or does it contain elements of conflict or change?

Example:

A protagonist in a desert landscape might feel isolated and introspective, searching for clarity and purpose amid the barren terrain.

3. The Call to Adventure

The call to adventure is the event or realization that disrupts the protagonist's ordinary world, compelling them to embark on their journey.

Types of Calls to Adventure:

- **External Event**: A life change, challenge, or opportunity that forces the protagonist to act.
- **Internal Realization**: A growing dissatisfaction, longing, or awareness that sparks the desire for transformation.

Example:

The protagonist discovers an ancient key (symbolizing untapped potential) hidden in their home, prompting them to uncover its purpose.

4. The Initial Conflict

Conflict introduces tension and sets the stakes for the journey. In the first chapter, this conflict often represents the protagonist's resistance to change or their encounter with the shadow.

Questions to Define the Conflict:

- What obstacle or challenge does the protagonist face at the start of their journey?
- How does this conflict reflect their inner struggles or fears?
- What is at stake if the protagonist fails to answer the call?

Example:

The protagonist hesitates to use the ancient key, fearing that it might unlock painful memories or bring unwanted responsibilities.

5. Themes and Motifs

The first chapter establishes the overarching themes and motifs that will recur throughout the myth. These elements provide depth and coherence to your narrative.

Examples of Themes:

- Transformation and growth.
- Light and shadow.
- Connection and isolation.

Examples of Motifs:

- Journeys or paths.
- Cycles of destruction and renewal.
- Symbols of guidance, such as stars or lanterns.

Writing the First Chapter: A Step-by-Step Guide
Follow these steps to craft the first chapter of your mythic journey:
Step 1: Begin with a Vivid Scene
Start your chapter with a moment that immerses the reader in your symbolic world. This scene should capture the mood, themes, and challenges of your journey.
Techniques for Starting Strong:

- **Describe the Setting**: Use sensory details to bring your symbolic world to life.
- **Introduce Action**: Begin with a significant event or decision that engages the protagonist.
- **Use Symbolism**: Incorporate a meaningful object, image, or motif to set the tone.

Example:
The chapter opens with the protagonist standing at the edge of a cliff, gazing at a distant mountain shrouded in mist, symbolizing an unclear but compelling future.
Step 2: Introduce the Protagonist
Introduce your mythic role and establish the protagonist's connection to the setting and situation.
Details to Include:

- Physical or symbolic descriptions that reflect the protagonist's traits.
- Internal thoughts or emotions that reveal their current state.
- Subtle hints at the protagonist's fears or aspirations.

Example:
The protagonist wears a weathered cloak, symbolizing both their resilience and the burdens they carry.
Step 3: Present the Call to Adventure
Reveal the event or realization that disrupts the protagonist's ordinary world and invites them to begin their journey.
Writing Tips:

- Create a sense of urgency or inevitability around the call.
- Show the protagonist's initial reaction, whether it's resistance, curiosity, or excitement.
- Use the call to introduce a key symbol or motif.

Example:
A messenger delivers a cryptic map that only the protagonist can decipher, representing their unique role in the unfolding story.

Step 4: Highlight the Initial Conflict

Introduce the first obstacle or shadow element that challenges the protagonist. This conflict sets the stage for growth and establishes the stakes of the journey.

Examples of Initial Conflicts:

- An external challenge, such as a rival or natural disaster.
- An internal struggle, such as doubt, fear, or resistance to change.

Example:

The protagonist encounters a guardian at the edge of the forest who demands that they confront their deepest fear before entering.

Step 5: End with a Hook

Conclude your chapter with a moment of tension or revelation that propels the story forward.

Techniques for Ending Strong:

- **Cliffhanger**: Leave the protagonist on the brink of a decision or action.
- **Foreshadowing**: Hint at challenges or discoveries yet to come.
- **Symbolic Gesture**: End with a meaningful action or image that encapsulates the chapter's themes.

Example:

The protagonist takes their first step into the shadowy forest, the ancient key glowing faintly in their hand.

Bringing Your First Chapter to Life

Once you've written your first chapter, revisit it to refine the narrative, deepen the symbolism, and ensure it reflects your authentic voice.

Questions for Revision:

- Does the chapter clearly introduce the protagonist, setting, and themes?
- Are the symbols and motifs integrated meaningfully into the narrative?
- Does the call to adventure feel compelling and aligned with your personal mythology?
- Does the chapter end with a sense of momentum and possibility?

Moving Forward: Expanding Your Myth

The first chapter of your myth is just the beginning. It serves as a foundation for the journey ahead, providing a framework for growth, exploration, and transformation. As you continue to write, let your archetypes, symbols, and motifs guide you, weaving a story that reflects the depth and complexity of your inner world.

Reflection Questions:

- How can I build on the themes and conflicts introduced in the first chapter?

- What new challenges, allies, or revelations might the protagonist encounter?
- How does this chapter set the stage for the protagonist's ultimate transformation?

Part 4: Living the Myth

Chapter 16: Embodying Your Myth: Rituals and Practices for Integration

Writing and visualizing your mythic journey is a powerful process of self-discovery, but its true transformation comes when you embody your myth. Embodiment means integrating the symbols, archetypes, and themes of your personal mythology into your daily life, making them a living, breathing part of your reality. Through intentional rituals and practices, you can align your actions with your mythic narrative, fostering growth, resilience, and authenticity.

This chapter explores the concept of embodying your myth, the importance of rituals for integration, and a range of practices that help bring your story into your lived experience. Whether through symbolic actions, mindfulness, or creative expression, embodying your myth bridges the gap between imagination and reality, empowering you to live a meaningful and intentional life.

Why Embody Your Myth?

When you embody your myth, you honor your journey by aligning your actions, choices, and behaviors with your inner truths. This integration transforms abstract concepts into tangible experiences, deepening your connection to your personal mythology.

Key Benefits of Embodying Your Myth:

1. **Self-Alignment**: Align your daily life with your values, aspirations, and inner narrative.
2. **Empowerment**: Recognize and activate your strengths, archetypes, and symbols.
3. **Resilience**: Use your mythic tools and motifs to navigate challenges with confidence.
4. **Creativity**: Bring your story to life through dynamic, expressive practices.
5. **Connection**: Strengthen your relationship with yourself and others through shared meaning.

The Role of Rituals in Integration

Rituals provide a structured way to embody your myth. They create sacred space and intentional moments for reflection, transformation, and action, allowing you to engage with your inner world in a tangible way.

What Is a Ritual?

A ritual is a deliberate act or series of actions imbued with symbolic meaning. It can be simple or elaborate, personal or communal, but its purpose is to honor, reinforce, or transform an aspect of your experience.

Examples of Rituals:

- Lighting a candle to signify a new beginning.
- Meditating on a symbolic object, such as a key or compass.
- Journaling as a dialogue with your archetypes or shadow.

Why Rituals Are Powerful:

1. **Symbolic Action**: Rituals externalize inner intentions, making them real and actionable.
2. **Focus and Presence**: They create a space for mindfulness and reflection.
3. **Transformation**: Repeated rituals reinforce change and growth over time.

Practices for Embodying Your Myth

Below are detailed rituals and practices to help you integrate your myth into your daily life. Choose those that resonate most with your journey and adapt them as needed.

1. Morning Myth Ritual: Begin Your Day with Intention

Start your day by connecting with your mythic narrative. This practice sets the tone for a purposeful and aligned day.

Steps:

1. **Sacred Space**: Designate a small area with meaningful objects (e.g., a candle, a symbol of your archetype).
2. **Visualization**: Spend 5–10 minutes visualizing your mythic world and protagonist. Reflect on your current place in the journey.
3. **Set an Intention**: Identify one action or mindset for the day that aligns with your mythic themes. For example:
   ◦ If you embody the Explorer, focus on curiosity and trying something new.
   ◦ If you embody the Caregiver, seek opportunities to nurture yourself or others.
4. **Symbolic Action**: Light a candle, hold a talisman, or recite an affirmation to seal your intention.

2. Seasonal or Monthly Rituals: Align with Cycles

Your mythic journey, like nature, unfolds in cycles. Create rituals that align with seasonal or monthly changes to honor your growth and transformation.

Examples:

• **Winter**: Reflect on themes of stillness, shadow work, and renewal. Write about lessons learned during times of introspection.
• **Spring**: Embrace themes of growth and rebirth by planting seeds, both literal and symbolic, to represent new intentions.
• **Full Moon**: Use the full moon to release what no longer serves your journey and reaffirm your path forward.

Exercise: Create a symbolic calendar where you map out key milestones, transitions, or moments to honor your journey with rituals.

3. Shadow Work Ritual: Embrace and Integrate the Shadow

Shadow work is an essential part of embodying your myth, as it allows you to confront and integrate hidden aspects of yourself.

Steps:

1. **Prepare a Symbol**: Choose an object or image that represents a shadow aspect you're working to integrate.
2. **Reflection**: Write or meditate on the shadow's lessons, challenges, and potential gifts.
3. **Symbolic Transformation**: Perform an act that symbolizes transformation, such as burning a piece of paper with limiting beliefs or placing a symbol of your shadow in a sacred space to honor its role in your growth.
4. **Affirmation**: Speak words of acceptance, such as, "I honor this part of myself and welcome its wisdom."

4. Creative Practices: Express Your Myth

Engage with your mythic journey through creative expression, turning abstract themes into tangible works of art.

Ideas:

- **Writing**: Journal or write poetry from the perspective of your archetypes or mythic characters.
- **Drawing or Painting**: Create visual representations of your symbols, landscapes, or motifs.
- **Music or Dance**: Compose or move to music that reflects the emotions and themes of your mythic journey.
- **Storytelling**: Share parts of your myth with others through spoken word, blogs, or performances.

5. Rituals of Gratitude: Honor the Journey

Gratitude rituals help you reflect on progress, acknowledge challenges, and celebrate growth.

Steps:

1. **Reflection**: At the end of the day or week, reflect on moments that aligned with your mythic journey.
2. **Gratitude Offering**: Write down or speak aloud three things you're grateful for in your story, such as an archetype's guidance, a lesson learned, or an unexpected opportunity.
3. **Symbolic Gesture**: Light incense, pour water into a special bowl, or create a small offering to honor the forces guiding your journey.

6. Guided Visualizations: Explore Your Mythic World

Guided visualizations allow you to immerse yourself in your mythic world, deepening your connection to its symbols and lessons.

Exercise:

1. **Create a Safe Space**: Sit in a quiet, comfortable location and close your eyes.
2. **Journey Visualization**: Imagine walking through your mythic landscape, encountering symbols, characters, or events. Pay attention to emotions and insights.
3. **Dialogue**: Engage with an archetype or shadow figure. Ask questions and listen for responses.
4. **Integration**: Journal about your experience and consider how it applies to your life.

7. Ritual Objects: Anchor Your Myth

Designate physical objects as symbols of your mythic journey. These items serve as reminders of your intentions and growth.

Examples of Ritual Objects:

- A piece of jewelry representing an archetype (e.g., a ring for the Ruler).
- A notebook or journal as your "Book of Myths."
- A crystal or talisman associated with a specific symbol or motif.

Practice: Carry or display these objects to stay connected to your journey throughout the day.

Sustaining Your Practices

Rituals and practices are most effective when they are consistent and adaptable. Over time, your needs and mythic journey will evolve, and your practices should reflect these changes.

Tips for Sustaining Rituals:

1. **Start Small**: Begin with simple practices and expand them as you feel comfortable.
2. **Be Flexible**: Adapt your rituals to fit your schedule, energy, and current challenges.
3. **Reflect Often**: Periodically review your practices to ensure they align with your growth and intentions.
4. **Celebrate Milestones**: Acknowledge progress in your mythic journey through special rituals or ceremonies.

Moving Forward: Living as the Hero of Your Myth

Embodying your myth transforms your personal mythology into a lived experience. Through rituals and practices, you not only honor your journey but actively shape it, aligning your daily life with your deepest values and aspirations. Each action becomes a step on your path, each moment a chapter in your evolving story.

Reflection Questions:

- What rituals or practices resonate most with my mythic journey?
- How can I integrate these practices into my daily life?
- How do I feel when I actively embody my myth?

Chapter 17: Facing the Trials: Challenges as Catalysts for Growth

No mythic journey is complete without trials—those pivotal moments of difficulty and transformation that test the hero's resolve, uncover hidden strengths, and propel them toward growth. Trials are not merely obstacles; they are opportunities to confront your fears, integrate your shadow, and refine your sense of purpose. Each challenge is a turning point that offers wisdom and clarity when met with courage and resilience.

In this chapter, we will explore the role of trials in your personal mythology, the archetypal significance of challenges, and practical strategies for navigating them. By reframing difficulties as catalysts for growth, you can face your trials with intention, learn from them, and emerge stronger and more self-aware.

The Role of Trials in Myth and Life

In mythology, trials are moments when the hero is tested—physically, emotionally, and spiritually. These tests often appear as external conflicts, internal struggles, or encounters with the unknown. In life, trials serve a similar purpose, forcing you to confront limitations, embrace change, and discover your resilience.

Key Functions of Trials:

1. **Reveal Strengths**: Challenges uncover hidden abilities and inner resources.
2. **Expose Shadows**: Trials bring repressed fears, insecurities, and beliefs to the surface for integration.
3. **Forge Transformation**: Facing difficulties catalyzes growth, reshaping your identity and perspective.
4. **Clarify Purpose**: Trials often serve as crossroads, prompting you to reflect on your goals and values.

Types of Trials: External and Internal

Trials take many forms, but they can generally be categorized as external or internal. Both are equally significant and often intertwined.

1. External Trials

External trials are challenges that arise from your environment, relationships, or circumstances. They test your ability to adapt, persevere, and assert your agency in the face of adversity.

Examples of External Trials:

- Career setbacks or financial difficulties.
- Conflicts with friends, family, or colleagues.
- Unexpected life changes, such as relocation, illness, or loss.

Significance: External trials mirror internal struggles, often highlighting areas where growth or healing is needed.

2. Internal Trials

Internal trials are struggles within your own psyche—fears, doubts, insecurities, or limiting beliefs. These challenges often emerge during moments of introspection or transition.

Examples of Internal Trials:

- Fear of failure or rejection.
- Overcoming perfectionism or procrastination.
- Facing unresolved trauma or grief.

Significance: Internal trials push you to confront and integrate aspects of yourself that have been ignored or suppressed.

Archetypal Themes in Trials

Trials often align with archetypal themes, reflecting universal patterns of growth and transformation. Recognizing these themes can help you frame your challenges within a broader context.

Common Archetypal Themes:

1. **The Descent into Darkness**: Entering the unknown to face fears or uncover hidden truths.
2. **The Test of Worthiness**: Proving your resolve, courage, or commitment to your path.
3. **The Battle with the Shadow**: Confronting repressed aspects of yourself or externalized fears.
4. **The Trial by Fire**: Enduring hardship to emerge transformed, like the phoenix rising from ashes.

Navigating Trials: A Step-by-Step Guide

Facing trials requires courage, preparation, and a willingness to learn. Below is a detailed guide to help you navigate challenges as catalysts for growth.

Step 1: Recognize the Trial

The first step is acknowledging that you are in a trial. Often, challenges are disguised as routine difficulties, but recognizing their significance allows you to approach them with intention.

Signs of a Trial:

- You feel stretched beyond your comfort zone.
- A recurring pattern or issue resurfaces in your life.
- You are faced with a decision or conflict that feels pivotal.

Exercise:

Journal about a current challenge. Reflect on how it aligns with the themes and motifs of your mythic journey. Consider what this trial might be teaching you.

Step 2: Reframe the Challenge

Reframing involves shifting your perspective on the trial, seeing it not as an obstacle but as an opportunity for growth.

Questions to Reframe a Trial:

- What lesson or insight might this challenge offer?
- How does this trial align with my goals or values?
- What strengths or resources can I draw upon to face it?

Example:

Instead of viewing a career setback as a failure, reframe it as a chance to reassess your direction and pursue opportunities that align more closely with your aspirations.

Step 3: Identify the Shadow

Trials often reveal shadow aspects—repressed fears, desires, or beliefs—that influence your actions and reactions. Identifying these shadows helps you integrate them into your conscious awareness.

Exercise:

Reflect on the emotions or thoughts triggered by the trial. Ask yourself:

- What am I afraid of in this situation?
- What does this trial reveal about my unmet needs or unresolved wounds?
- How can I acknowledge and work with this shadow?

Step 4: Break Down the Challenge

Large trials can feel overwhelming. Breaking them into smaller, manageable steps helps you maintain focus and build momentum.

Steps for Breaking Down a Trial:

1. Define the core issue or problem.
2. Identify actionable steps to address it.
3. Set small, achievable goals for each step.
4. Celebrate progress, no matter how small.

Example:

If the trial involves a major life transition, such as moving to a new city, break it down into steps like researching neighborhoods, finding housing, and building a local support network.

Step 5: Engage Your Archetypes

Call upon the strengths of your archetypes to help you navigate the trial. Each archetype offers unique qualities and perspectives that can support you.

Examples:

- **The Hero**: Embody courage and determination to face the trial head-on.
- **The Sage**: Seek wisdom and guidance to gain clarity and insight.
- **The Caregiver**: Practice self-compassion and nurture yourself through the process.

Exercise:

Write a dialogue with one of your archetypes, asking for their advice or perspective on the trial. Reflect on their response and how you can apply it.

Step 6: Practice Resilience and Adaptability

Resilience is the ability to endure and recover from challenges, while adaptability allows you to adjust your approach as circumstances change.

Techniques for Building Resilience:

- **Mindfulness**: Stay present and grounded, focusing on what you can control.
- **Affirmations**: Repeat empowering statements, such as, "I am strong enough to overcome this."
- **Support Systems**: Lean on friends, family, or mentors for encouragement and guidance.

Techniques for Adaptability:

- Stay open to new solutions or perspectives.
- View setbacks as opportunities to pivot and try a different approach.
- Reflect on past challenges and how you successfully navigated them.

Step 7: Reflect and Integrate

After facing a trial, take time to reflect on what you've learned and how you've grown. Integration solidifies the lessons and prepares you for future challenges.

Reflection Questions:

- What did I learn about myself through this trial?
- How have my strengths, values, or archetypes evolved?
- How can I apply these lessons to other areas of my life?

Exercise:

Write a journal entry or create a piece of art that symbolizes the trial and its outcome. Use this as a reminder of your resilience and growth.

Turning Trials into Triumphs

When you approach trials as catalysts for growth, you transform challenges into opportunities for empowerment. Each trial you face adds depth and richness to your mythic journey, shaping you into a more resilient and authentic version of yourself.

Key Takeaways:

1. Trials are not obstacles but opportunities for transformation.
2. External challenges mirror internal struggles, offering insight into your inner world.
3. Reframing, shadow work, and archetypal support are essential tools for navigating trials.
4. Reflection and integration turn difficult experiences into lasting wisdom.

Moving Forward: Embracing Future Trials

As your journey continues, new trials will inevitably arise. Approach them with curiosity, courage, and trust in your ability to grow. Remember that each challenge is a stepping stone toward greater self-awareness, strength, and fulfillment.

Reflection Questions:

- How have past trials shaped who I am today?
- What current challenges can I reframe as opportunities for growth?
- How can I use my mythic tools and practices to face future trials with confidence?

Chapter 18: Allies and Adversaries: Identifying Key Figures in Your Story

No mythic journey unfolds in isolation. Along the way, every hero encounters allies who provide guidance, support, and encouragement, as well as adversaries who challenge, test, or obstruct their progress. These key figures—whether external individuals or internal archetypes—are integral to the story, helping to shape the protagonist's growth and transformation.

In this chapter, we will explore the roles of allies and adversaries in your personal mythology, how to identify them, and how to engage with their lessons. You'll learn to recognize the people, patterns, and archetypes that influence your journey, empowering you to build meaningful relationships and navigate conflicts with intention.

The Role of Allies and Adversaries in Myth and Life

In mythology, allies and adversaries serve as mirrors and catalysts for the hero. They reflect aspects of the hero's strengths and weaknesses, provide opportunities for growth, and propel the narrative forward. In your life, allies and adversaries function similarly, influencing your choices, challenges, and triumphs.

Allies:

Allies are figures who support the hero, offering wisdom, resources, or companionship. They may serve as mentors, friends, or collaborators, helping the hero to navigate trials and achieve their goals.

Adversaries:

Adversaries are figures or forces that oppose the hero, creating conflict and resistance. They test the hero's resolve, uncover hidden fears or limitations, and often represent aspects of the shadow.

Both allies and adversaries are essential to your story, as they reveal different facets of your character and propel you toward self-discovery and growth.

Identifying Allies: The Supporters of Your Journey

Allies can take many forms, from trusted friends and mentors to symbolic or spiritual guides. Recognizing your allies involves reflecting on the people and forces that uplift and empower you.

Types of Allies

1. **The Mentor**
   - **Role**: Provides wisdom, guidance, and inspiration.
   - **Example**: A teacher who shares valuable knowledge or a mentor who helps you navigate a career path.
   - **Mythic Example**: Gandalf in *The Lord of the Rings* or Obi-Wan Kenobi in *Star Wars*.
2. **The Companion**
   - **Role**: Offers emotional support and companionship.
   - **Example**: A close friend or partner who stands by you through challenges.
   - **Mythic Example**: Samwise Gamgee in *The Lord of the Rings*.
3. **The Catalyst**
   - **Role**: Inspires or motivates you to take action, often through their own example or encouragement.
   - **Example**: A peer who challenges you to step out of your comfort zone.
   - **Mythic Example**: The Muse in Greek mythology, sparking creativity.
4. **The Protector**
   - **Role**: Shields you from harm or provides a sense of safety.
   - **Example**: A parent, guardian, or close confidant who advocates for your well-being.
   - **Mythic Example**: Hagrid in *Harry Potter*.
5. **The Inner Ally**
   - **Role**: Represents an internal archetype or trait that supports your growth, such as courage, intuition, or resilience.
   - **Example**: The part of you that motivates you to keep going despite fear.
   - **Mythic Example**: The hero's inner voice or guiding instinct.

Identifying Your Allies
Reflection Questions:

1. Who in my life provides support, encouragement, or guidance?
2. What traits or qualities do my allies embody?
3. Are there internal strengths or archetypes that I can rely on as allies?
4. How have my allies helped me overcome challenges or achieve goals?

Exercise:

- Create a "Circle of Allies" by listing the people, archetypes, or forces that have positively influenced your journey. Reflect on how each has contributed to your growth.

Identifying Adversaries: The Forces That Challenge You

Adversaries in your story are not merely villains—they are agents of transformation. They force you to confront your fears, question your beliefs, and rise to meet challenges. Recognizing your adversaries involves examining the people, situations, or internal conflicts that test you.

Types of Adversaries

1. **The Opponent**
   - **Role**: Directly opposes your goals or creates obstacles.
   - **Example**: A rival at work or a difficult relationship that challenges your boundaries.
   - **Mythic Example**: Darth Vader in *Star Wars*.
2. **The Tempter**
   - **Role**: Attempts to lure you away from your path through distraction or false promises.
   - **Example**: A situation or person that tempts you to compromise your values.
   - **Mythic Example**: The Sirens in Greek mythology.
3. **The Shadow Figure**
   - **Role**: Represents repressed fears, insecurities, or aspects of the self that you must confront.
   - **Example**: A recurring pattern of self-doubt or negative self-talk.
   - **Mythic Example**: The doppelgänger or dark reflection of the hero.
4. **The Chaos Bringer**
   - **Role**: Creates disruption or unpredictability, forcing you to adapt.
   - **Example**: A life-changing event, such as a sudden loss or unexpected challenge.
   - **Mythic Example**: Loki in Norse mythology.
5. **The Inner Adversary**
   - **Role**: Represents internal resistance, such as fear, procrastination, or limiting beliefs.
   - **Example**: The part of you that sabotages progress or avoids discomfort.
   - **Mythic Example**: The hero's doubt before taking the leap.

Identifying Your Adversaries
Reflection Questions:

1. Who or what creates conflict, resistance, or challenges in my life?
2. What fears or limitations do my adversaries reflect?
3. Are there internal patterns or beliefs that act as adversaries?
4. How have my adversaries helped me grow, even unintentionally?

Exercise:

- Create an "Adversary Map" by listing the external and internal forces that challenge you. Reflect on how each has shaped your journey.

Engaging with Allies and Adversaries

Allies and adversaries are not static—they are dynamic forces that evolve as your story progresses. Engaging with them intentionally helps you harness their lessons and integrate their influence into your growth.

Engaging with Allies

1. **Strengthen Connections**: Invest time and energy in relationships with allies, whether they are people, archetypes, or spiritual guides.
2. **Ask for Guidance**: Seek advice or support from allies when facing challenges.
3. **Acknowledge Contributions**: Express gratitude for the role your allies play in your journey.
4. **Embody Ally Traits**: Reflect on the qualities your allies possess and how you can cultivate them in yourself.

Exercise: Write a letter to one of your allies (real or symbolic) expressing gratitude for their support and reflecting on what they've taught you.

Engaging with Adversaries

1. **Reframe Adversaries as Teachers**: View challenges and conflicts as opportunities for growth rather than obstacles.
2. **Confront with Compassion**: Address adversaries—both external and internal—with understanding and courage.
3. **Identify the Lesson**: Reflect on what the adversary reveals about your fears, limitations, or strengths.
4. **Set Boundaries**: Protect your energy and well-being by establishing boundaries with adversaries that no longer serve your growth.

Exercise:

- Write about a conflict or challenge involving an adversary. Reflect on what it taught you and how it contributed to your development.

The Interplay of Allies and Adversaries

Allies and adversaries are interconnected, often reflecting different aspects of the same lessons. For example, a supportive mentor might challenge you to push beyond your limits, acting as both an ally and an adversary. Similarly, an adversary may inadvertently inspire growth or reveal hidden strengths, transforming into an unexpected ally.

Reflection Questions:

1. Are there adversaries in my life who have also acted as allies?
2. How do my allies and adversaries complement each other in my story?
3. What balance do I see between support and challenge in my journey?

Moving Forward: Building Relationships in Your Myth

As your journey continues, new allies and adversaries will emerge, shaping your story in unexpected ways. Embrace these figures with curiosity and openness, recognizing their role in your growth.

Key Takeaways:

- Allies provide guidance, support, and encouragement, empowering you to move forward.
- Adversaries create resistance and conflict, challenging you to confront fears and grow.
- Both allies and adversaries are essential to your myth, offering complementary lessons and opportunities for transformation.

Reflection Questions:

- Who are the current allies and adversaries in my life?
- How can I strengthen my relationships with allies?
- What lessons can I learn from my adversaries?

Chapter 19: Rebirth and Renewal: Rewriting Your Myth Over Time

Every myth, like life itself, is a dynamic story. It evolves, adapts, and transforms as its hero grows and changes. Rebirth and renewal are essential themes in mythology and personal development, symbolizing the cycles of death and transformation that define our journey. These moments of rewriting your myth represent opportunities to shed old identities, beliefs, and patterns, allowing you to emerge with greater clarity, purpose, and authenticity.

In this chapter, we will explore the concept of rebirth and renewal within your personal mythology. We'll examine the reasons for rewriting your myth, the symbolic significance of cycles, and practical steps for embracing transformation. By learning to revise your myth intentionally, you can navigate life's transitions with grace, resilience, and empowerment.

The Nature of Rebirth in Myth and Life

Rebirth is a recurring motif in mythology, representing the hero's ability to overcome trials, transcend limitations, and emerge transformed. In your life, moments of rebirth often follow periods of crisis, reflection, or profound change, marking the transition from one chapter to the next.

Key Characteristics of Rebirth:

1. **Release**: Letting go of old identities, attachments, or beliefs that no longer serve you.
2. **Transformation**: Emerging with a renewed sense of self, purpose, or perspective.
3. **Integration**: Honoring the lessons of the past while embracing new possibilities.

Examples of Mythic Rebirth:

- **The Phoenix**: Rising from the ashes, the phoenix symbolizes resilience and renewal.
- **The Seasons**: The cycle of death in winter and rebirth in spring reflects nature's perpetual renewal.
- **The Hero's Return**: In the hero's journey, the return home often signifies the hero's transformation and readiness to share their newfound wisdom.

Why Rewrite Your Myth?

Rewriting your myth is an act of empowerment, allowing you to align your story with your evolving identity, values, and goals. It acknowledges that change is a natural and necessary part of growth.

Reasons to Rewrite Your Myth:

1. **Life Transitions**: Major events such as career changes, relationships, or relocations may require a new narrative.
2. **Personal Growth**: As you discover new aspects of yourself, your myth must evolve to reflect your expanded awareness.
3. **Overcoming Limitations**: Old stories that reinforce fear, doubt, or stagnation must be rewritten to support progress.
4. **Healing**: Rewriting your myth can help you integrate past wounds, transforming them into sources of strength and wisdom.

The Symbolism of Cycles: Embracing Change

Cycles are fundamental to life and mythology, reminding us that endings are not final but transitions into new beginnings. By embracing the cyclical nature of your journey, you can approach rebirth with trust and openness.

Key Cycles in Myth and Life:

1. **The Hero's Journey**: Departure, initiation, and return form a continuous loop of growth and renewal.
2. **The Seasons**: Spring, summer, autumn, and winter mirror the phases of birth, growth, decline, and renewal.
3. **The Moon Phases**: The waxing, full, and waning moon symbolize cycles of intention, culmination, and release.

Reflection Questions:

- What cycle am I currently experiencing in my life?
- How does this cycle invite me to release, grow, or renew?

Steps to Rewrite Your Myth

Rewriting your myth is a deliberate process of reflection, release, and reinvention. Below is a step-by-step guide to help you navigate this transformation.

Step 1: Reflect on Your Current Story

Begin by examining the narrative you are currently living. This includes your beliefs, values, and the roles you play in your life.

Questions for Reflection:

- What story am I telling about myself right now?
- How does this story serve or limit me?
- What aspects of this story feel outdated or misaligned with my true self?

Exercise:

Write a summary of your current myth. Highlight the parts that resonate with your authentic self and those that feel like they need to change.

Step 2: Identify What Needs to Be Released

Rebirth requires releasing what no longer serves you. This could include old beliefs, habits, or roles that prevent you from moving forward.

Questions for Release:

- What patterns or behaviors am I ready to let go of?
- Are there relationships or roles that no longer align with my journey?
- What fears or doubts am I ready to release?

Exercise:

Write a "Release Letter" to symbolize letting go. Address it to the parts of your story you're ready to leave behind, thanking them for their lessons and saying goodbye.

Step 3: Define Your New Story

After releasing the old, envision the myth you want to create. This new story should reflect your current values, aspirations, and sense of self.

Questions for Visioning:

- What do I want my new story to focus on?
- What archetypes or roles do I want to embody?
- What symbols or themes will guide my journey moving forward?

Exercise:

Write the first chapter of your new myth, describing the protagonist (you), the setting, and the goals or themes of this new phase of life.

Step 4: Anchor Your New Story in Symbols and Rituals

Symbols and rituals help solidify your new story, making it a tangible part of your life.

Examples of Anchors:

- **Symbolic Objects:** Choose a new object (e.g., a piece of jewelry, a crystal, or a journal) to represent your rebirth.
- **Rituals of Renewal:** Create a personal ceremony to honor your transition, such as lighting a candle, planting a seed, or taking a symbolic journey.
- **Affirmations:** Write affirmations that reflect your new story and repeat them daily.

Step 5: Integrate the Lessons of the Past

Rebirth does not mean discarding the past; it involves integrating its lessons into your new story. This process honors where you've been while focusing on where you're going.

Reflection Questions:

- What have I learned from the challenges and successes of my past?
- How can these lessons guide my new story?
- What strengths or values have emerged from my experiences?

Exercise:

Create a "Lessons Map" by listing key moments from your past and the wisdom they've provided. Reflect on how these lessons inform your new narrative.

Step 6: Embody Your New Myth

Finally, live your new story with intention and authenticity. Embodying your myth means aligning your actions, choices, and mindset with your renewed narrative.

Tips for Embodying Your Myth:

1. **Act in Alignment:** Make choices that reflect your new story and its values.
2. **Revisit and Refine:** Periodically review your myth to ensure it evolves with you.
3. **Celebrate Progress:** Honor milestones and achievements that reflect your transformation.

Examples of Rebirth in Personal Myths

To inspire your process, here are examples of how rebirth might appear in personal mythology:

1. **From Victim to Survivor:** A narrative of helplessness transforms into one of resilience and empowerment.
2. **From Wanderer to Explorer:** A period of uncertainty becomes a journey of curiosity and discovery.
3. **From Healer to Teacher:** A focus on personal healing evolves into a desire to guide others.

Moving Forward: Embracing Cycles of Renewal

Rebirth is not a one-time event but an ongoing process. Each cycle of renewal brings you closer to your true self, allowing your myth to reflect the depth and complexity of your journey.

Key Takeaways:

- Rebirth involves releasing the old, envisioning the new, and integrating the lessons of the past.
- Cycles of transformation are natural and necessary for growth.
- Rewriting your myth is an act of empowerment, aligning your narrative with your evolving self.

Reflection Questions:

- What aspects of my story am I ready to rewrite?
- How can I honor the themes of rebirth and renewal in my life?
- What steps can I take today to begin living my new myth?

Chapter 20: Aligning Myth with Reality: Bridging Inner and Outer Worlds

A myth is not merely a story—it is a lens through which you view the world, make decisions, and find meaning. Aligning your myth with reality means integrating the lessons, symbols, and archetypes of your personal mythology into your daily life. It is about creating harmony between your inner journey and the external world, ensuring that your actions reflect your values, your story guides your choices, and your life becomes an authentic expression of your mythic narrative.

In this chapter, we will explore how to bridge the gap between the inner and outer worlds. We'll examine the importance of aligning myth with reality, practical steps for integration, and how to navigate the challenges of living authentically. By connecting your mythic story to the tangible aspects of your life, you can create a purposeful and fulfilling existence.

The Importance of Aligning Myth with Reality

Your personal mythology reflects your deepest truths—your values, aspirations, and sense of purpose. However, if your external life does not align with this inner narrative, it can create tension, dissatisfaction, and a sense of disconnection. Aligning myth with reality ensures that your outer world supports your inner growth, fostering balance and authenticity.

Benefits of Alignment:

1. **Clarity**: A unified inner and outer world provides a clear sense of direction.
2. **Authenticity**: Living in alignment with your myth allows you to express your true self.
3. **Resilience**: A cohesive story helps you navigate challenges with purpose and confidence.
4. **Fulfillment**: Integrating your myth into daily life creates a sense of meaning and joy.

Signs of Misalignment Between Myth and Reality

Misalignment occurs when your external actions, relationships, or environment are at odds with your inner values and story. Recognizing these signs is the first step toward bridging the gap.

Common Signs of Misalignment:

- **Dissatisfaction**: Feeling unfulfilled or disconnected from your work, relationships, or goals.
- **Conflict**: Experiencing tension between your desires and obligations.
- **Inauthenticity**: Acting in ways that do not reflect your true self or values.
- **Stagnation**: Feeling stuck or unable to progress toward your aspirations.

Reflection Questions:

- Are my daily actions aligned with my values and goals?
- Do my relationships support or hinder my personal growth?
- Am I living a life that feels true to my mythic narrative?

Steps to Align Myth with Reality

Bridging your inner and outer worlds requires deliberate action and reflection. The following steps provide a framework for creating alignment between your myth and your reality.

Step 1: Revisit Your Myth

Begin by revisiting your mythic narrative to ensure it reflects your current values, goals, and sense of self.

Questions for Reflection:

- What themes or symbols in my myth resonate most with my life right now?
- Are there aspects of my myth that need to evolve or adapt to my current reality?
- How does my myth guide my purpose and priorities?

Exercise: Write a brief summary of your myth, focusing on the protagonist's goals, challenges, and values. Use this as a foundation for aligning your external life.

Step 2: Assess Your Current Reality

Examine your external world to identify areas that align with your myth and those that require adjustment.

Areas to Assess:

- **Career**: Does your work reflect your values and aspirations?
- **Relationships**: Do your relationships support your growth and authenticity?
- **Environment**: Does your physical space inspire and align with your story?
- **Habits and Routines**: Do your daily actions reinforce your mythic goals?

Exercise: Create a "Reality Map" by listing key aspects of your life (e.g., career, relationships, health) and noting whether they align with your myth. Highlight areas for improvement.

Step 3: Identify Bridges Between Inner and Outer Worlds
Bridges are tangible actions or changes that connect your inner story to your external reality. These bridges help you embody your myth in practical and meaningful ways.
Examples of Bridges:

- **Symbols in Action**: If your myth involves growth (symbolized by a tree), plant something as a daily reminder of your journey.
- **Purposeful Choices**: Align your decisions with your values, such as choosing work that reflects your passion or purpose.
- **Creative Expression**: Use art, writing, or music to bring your mythic themes into your daily life.

Exercise: Identify one bridge for each area of your life that requires alignment. For example, if your career feels misaligned, consider how you can integrate your archetypes or values into your work.

Step 4: Create Rituals for Alignment
Rituals provide a structured way to connect your inner and outer worlds. They reinforce your mythic narrative and keep you grounded in your purpose.
Examples of Rituals:

- **Morning Intentions**: Begin each day with an intention that reflects your mythic goals.
- **Reflection Journaling**: Write about how your actions each day align with your story.
- **Monthly Reviews**: Reflect on your progress toward aligning myth and reality, adjusting as needed.

Exercise: Design a daily ritual that incorporates a key symbol, archetype, or value from your myth. For example, light a candle each morning to symbolize clarity and purpose.

Step 5: Address Barriers to Alignment
Challenges and resistance are natural when aligning your myth with reality. Identifying and addressing these barriers is crucial for sustained progress.
Common Barriers:

- **Fear of Change**: Resistance to letting go of comfort or familiarity.
- **External Expectations**: Pressure to conform to societal or relational expectations.
- **Self-Doubt**: Belief that you are not capable or deserving of living your myth.

Strategies for Overcoming Barriers:

1. **Reframe Fear**: View change as an opportunity for growth rather than a threat.
2. **Set Boundaries**: Protect your time, energy, and priorities from external pressures.
3. **Build Confidence**: Celebrate small wins and remind yourself of past successes.

Step 6: Embrace Continuous Adaptation

Alignment is not a one-time achievement but an ongoing process. As your myth evolves, so too must your external reality.

Tips for Continuous Adaptation:

- Regularly revisit and revise your myth to reflect your growth.
- Stay open to new opportunities, perspectives, and lessons.
- Celebrate progress, even when alignment feels incomplete.

Exercise: Set aside time each season to review your myth and reality. Reflect on what's working, what's not, and what needs adjustment.

Living an Aligned Life

When your myth and reality are in harmony, life feels purposeful, authentic, and fulfilling. Each action becomes a reflection of your inner journey, and each moment reinforces your sense of connection to your story.

Signs of Alignment:

- You feel a sense of flow and ease in your daily life.
- Your actions consistently reflect your values and aspirations.
- You experience greater resilience and clarity in navigating challenges.
- Your relationships and environment support your growth and authenticity.

Examples of Myth-Reality Alignment

1. **The Explorer Myth**: A protagonist values curiosity and discovery.
   - **Alignment**: Takes small trips, learns new skills, and embraces uncertainty in their career.
2. **The Caregiver Myth**: A protagonist prioritizes nurturing and connection.
   - **Alignment**: Builds meaningful relationships, volunteers, and creates a warm, welcoming home environment.
3. **The Sage Myth**: A protagonist seeks knowledge and wisdom.
   - **Alignment**: Pursues education, mentors others, and engages in reflective practices like meditation.

Moving Forward: Sustaining Alignment

Aligning your myth with reality is a lifelong practice. It requires ongoing reflection, intentional action, and a commitment to living authentically. As you continue your journey, trust in the power of your myth to guide you, and remember that alignment is not about perfection but about progress.

Reflection Questions:

- What small steps can I take today to align my actions with my story?
- How can I use rituals or symbols to stay connected to my myth?
- What lessons have I learned from aligning my inner and outer worlds?

\

Part 5: Sharing Your Myth

Chapter 21: Telling Your Story: Sharing Your Myth with the World

The act of telling your story is a powerful form of self-expression and connection. Sharing your myth allows you to inspire others, deepen your understanding of yourself, and contribute meaningfully to the collective human narrative. Your personal mythology, filled with triumphs, trials, and transformations, holds wisdom that others can resonate with and learn from. Telling your story is not just about recounting events—it is about distilling meaning, offering perspective, and illuminating the universal truths within your unique journey.

In this chapter, we will explore the importance of storytelling, the different ways you can share your myth, and how to overcome the challenges of vulnerability and self-doubt. By embracing the power of your story, you not only empower yourself but also create ripples of inspiration and connection in the world.

The Power of Storytelling

Storytelling is a fundamental human activity that transcends cultures, eras, and languages. It is how we make sense of the world, connect with others, and preserve our experiences. Sharing your story transforms your inner journey into an offering that can uplift, educate, or guide others.

Why Share Your Story?

1. **Inspire Others**: Your story can motivate others to face their challenges and pursue their dreams.
2. **Foster Connection**: Sharing your vulnerabilities and triumphs builds empathy and strengthens relationships.
3. **Promote Healing**: Telling your story can be cathartic, helping you process emotions and integrate lessons.
4. **Empower Yourself**: Owning and articulating your narrative reinforces your sense of agency and purpose.

Preparing to Share Your Myth

Before you share your story, it's important to reflect on your intentions, choose the right medium, and prepare for the process of storytelling. This preparation ensures that your narrative is authentic, impactful, and aligned with your goals.

Step 1: Clarify Your Intentions

Understanding why you want to share your story helps you frame it in a way that resonates with both you and your audience.

Questions for Reflection:

- What do I hope to achieve by sharing my story?
- Who is my intended audience?
- What key messages or lessons do I want to convey?

Examples of Intentions:

- **To Inspire:** Share how you overcame adversity to encourage others.
- **To Educate:** Use your experiences to teach others about a specific topic or journey.
- **To Connect:** Open up about your vulnerabilities to foster understanding and empathy.

Step 2: Choose Your Medium

Your myth can be shared through various forms, depending on your strengths, preferences, and audience. Each medium offers unique opportunities for expression.

Common Mediums for Storytelling:

1. **Writing:** Share your story through blogs, essays, memoirs, or fiction.
   - **Strengths:** Allows for detailed exploration and creative expression.
2. **Speaking:** Tell your story through public speaking, podcasts, or conversations.
   - **Strengths:** Engages audiences through tone, emotion, and presence.
3. **Art:** Use visual art, music, or performance to express your narrative.
   - **Strengths:** Evokes emotions and transcends language barriers.
4. **Social Media:** Share snippets of your journey through posts, videos, or reels.
   - **Strengths:** Reaches a broad audience and encourages interaction.

Exercise: Experiment with different mediums to discover which feels most natural and effective for conveying your story.

Step 3: Identify Key Themes and Moments

Focus your story on the themes and moments that are most meaningful and impactful. This helps create a coherent and engaging narrative.

Questions for Reflection:

- What are the major turning points in my story?
- What themes or motifs run consistently through my journey?
- How have I changed or grown as a result of these experiences?

Exercise: Outline your story, breaking it into key chapters or sections. For each, identify the central theme, key events, and lessons learned.

Step 4: Craft an Authentic Narrative

Authenticity is the cornerstone of impactful storytelling. Be honest about your experiences, emotions, and lessons, even if they involve vulnerability.

Tips for Crafting an Authentic Narrative:

1. **Use Your Voice**: Write or speak in a way that feels natural and true to you.
2. **Show, Don't Just Tell**: Use vivid details and examples to bring your story to life.
3. **Balance Vulnerability and Strength**: Share struggles and triumphs to create a balanced narrative.
4. **Include Lessons and Reflections**: Highlight what you've learned and how it has shaped you.

Example:

Instead of saying, "I faced a hard time," describe the specific challenges, how you felt, and what helped you overcome them.

Overcoming Challenges in Sharing Your Story

Sharing your myth can feel daunting, especially when it involves revealing personal or vulnerable aspects of your life. Addressing these challenges helps you share your story with confidence and courage.

Challenge 1: Fear of Judgment

Fear of being judged or misunderstood is a common barrier to storytelling. Reframing your perspective can help overcome this fear.

Reframe:

- Your story is not about pleasing everyone—it's about expressing your truth.
- Those who resonate with your story are the ones who need to hear it.

Affirmation: "I share my story with courage and authenticity, knowing it will reach those who need it."

Challenge 2: Self-Doubt

Doubting the value of your story can hold you back from sharing it. Recognize that every story, no matter how ordinary it may seem, has the power to inspire and connect.

Reflection:

- What aspects of my story might resonate with others?
- How has another person's story inspired or helped me?

Exercise: Write down three ways your story might positively impact others. Use this as motivation to share it.

Challenge 3: Emotional Vulnerability

Sharing deeply personal experiences can feel exposing. Setting boundaries and focusing on your purpose can help you navigate this vulnerability.

Tips for Managing Vulnerability:

- **Set Limits**: Share only what feels comfortable and necessary for your story.
- **Seek Support**: Share your story with trusted friends or mentors before presenting it to a broader audience.
- **Focus on Impact**: Remember that your vulnerability can create connection and inspire others.

Sharing Your Myth with the World

Once you are ready to share your story, approach it with intention and openness. Whether through a single conversation or a published work, your myth has the potential to create meaningful impact.

1. Engage Your Audience

Connect with your audience by making your story relatable and accessible. Highlight universal themes and emotions that resonate with others.

Tips:

- Use simple, clear language.
- Incorporate elements of humor, warmth, or hope to balance heavier themes.
- Invite feedback or dialogue to create a sense of connection.

2. Collaborate and Build Community

Sharing your myth can be a collaborative experience, fostering community and mutual growth. Seek opportunities to connect with others who share similar journeys or interests.

Ideas:

- Join storytelling groups, creative workshops, or online communities.
- Collaborate on projects that combine your story with others' narratives.
- Mentor or guide those who are inspired by your journey.

3. Adapt and Expand Your Story

As your life evolves, so does your myth. Embrace the fluid nature of storytelling, allowing your narrative to grow and adapt over time.

Reflection:

- How has my story changed since I first began telling it?
- What new themes, challenges, or lessons can I incorporate?

Exercise: Periodically update your story, adding new chapters or revising old ones to reflect your current journey.

The Ripple Effect: Inspiring Others Through Your Myth

When you share your story, its impact extends beyond yourself. Your myth becomes a source of guidance, hope, and inspiration for others, creating a ripple effect of transformation.

Key Takeaways:

- Your story has the power to change lives, including your own.
- Authenticity and vulnerability foster connection and trust.
- Sharing your myth is an act of courage, creativity, and generosity.

Reflection Questions:

- Who might benefit from hearing my story?
- How can I use my myth to inspire or support others?
- What legacy do I want my story to leave behind?

Moving Forward: Living and Sharing Your Myth

Sharing your myth is not just a single act—it is an ongoing process of connection, creativity, and growth. By telling your story with authenticity and purpose, you contribute to the collective human experience, inspiring others to embrace their own journeys.

Chapter 22: Inspiring Others: Myth as a Tool for Connection

Your personal myth is not only a reflection of your inner journey but also a powerful tool for inspiring and connecting with others. Myths have always served as bridges between individuals, offering shared symbols, values, and lessons that resonate across cultures and time. By sharing your myth, you create opportunities to foster understanding, inspire transformation, and build a community rooted in shared meaning.

In this chapter, we will explore how your personal myth can serve as a tool for connection. We'll examine the universal power of myths, strategies for inspiring others through your story, and ways to build meaningful relationships by aligning your myth with the collective experience. By using your myth as a source of connection, you contribute to a shared narrative that uplifts and empowers those around you.

The Universal Power of Myth

At their core, myths are not isolated stories—they are shared experiences that resonate on a universal level. Myths speak to the archetypes, emotions, and challenges that unite humanity, making them powerful tools for fostering connection.

Key Characteristics of Myths:

1. **Universality**: Myths address themes and emotions that transcend cultural and personal boundaries.
2. **Symbolism**: They use symbols to convey complex ideas in a way that is accessible and relatable.
3. **Guidance**: Myths provide a framework for navigating life's challenges and transitions.

Examples of Universal Themes in Myths:

- The hero's journey of transformation.
- The search for meaning and purpose.
- The interplay between light and shadow.

Reflection:

How does your personal myth reflect universal themes? What aspects of your story might resonate with others?

Why Inspire Others with Your Myth?

Sharing your myth is a deeply personal act, but its impact extends far beyond yourself. By inspiring others with your story, you create opportunities for growth, healing, and connection.

Benefits of Inspiring Others:

1. **Empowerment**: Your story can motivate others to take action, overcome obstacles, and pursue their dreams.
2. **Fostering Understanding**: Sharing your vulnerabilities and insights helps others feel seen and understood.
3. **Building Community**: Your myth becomes a point of connection, uniting people with shared experiences or aspirations.
4. **Catalyzing Change**: By sharing your lessons, you contribute to the collective growth and transformation of those around you.

Strategies for Inspiring Others Through Your Myth

Inspiring others begins with intentional storytelling and authentic expression. The following strategies can help you share your myth in a way that resonates and connects.

1. Focus on Relatable Themes

Relatability is key to connecting with others through your myth. By highlighting universal emotions, challenges, and triumphs, you create a narrative that others can see themselves in.

Tips for Highlighting Relatable Themes:

- Identify the core emotions in your story, such as fear, hope, or resilience.
- Focus on the lessons or insights that emerged from your experiences.
- Use accessible language and examples to make your story approachable.

Example:

If your myth centers on overcoming self-doubt, frame it around the universal struggle to believe in oneself and pursue personal growth.

2. Be Vulnerable and Authentic

Authenticity creates trust and connection. By sharing your struggles, fears, and imperfections, you invite others to connect with your humanity.

Tips for Authentic Storytelling:

- Share both your challenges and triumphs to create a balanced narrative.
- Avoid over-polishing your story—let your voice and perspective shine through.
- Be honest about your ongoing growth and the lessons you are still learning.

Example:

Instead of presenting your story as a flawless journey, share moments of uncertainty or failure and how you navigated them.

3. Incorporate Symbolism and Metaphor

Symbols and metaphors add depth and resonance to your myth, helping others connect with its meaning on an emotional level.

Examples of Symbolic Language:

- Use metaphors like "climbing a mountain" to describe overcoming challenges.
- Incorporate archetypes, such as the hero or mentor, to frame your journey.
- Highlight personal symbols, such as a compass or lantern, to represent your guiding values.

Exercise:

Identify key symbols in your myth and explore how they might resonate with others. Use these symbols to add depth to your storytelling.

4. Invite Reflection and Engagement

Inspiring others is not just about sharing your story—it's about encouraging them to reflect on their own journeys. Create opportunities for your audience to connect your story to their experiences.

Ways to Encourage Engagement:

- Ask reflective questions, such as, "What challenges in your life mirror this journey?"
- Offer prompts for journaling or discussion based on themes in your myth.
- Create interactive experiences, such as workshops, where participants can explore their own narratives.

Example:

If your myth focuses on transformation, invite others to share moments when they experienced significant growth or change.

5. Use Multiple Mediums

Different mediums allow you to reach diverse audiences and express your myth in various ways. Experiment with formats to find what resonates most with your audience.

Examples of Mediums:

- **Visual Art**: Create paintings, drawings, or digital art that represent themes from your myth.
- **Writing**: Share your story through blog posts, essays, or books.
- **Speaking**: Host webinars, podcasts, or live events to share your journey.
- **Social Media**: Use platforms like Instagram, TikTok, or Twitter to share snippets of your myth.

Exercise:

Choose one new medium to experiment with and create a piece that represents a key aspect of your myth.

Building Relationships Through Shared Myths

Sharing your myth is a collaborative process that can strengthen relationships and build community. By inviting others to share their stories, you create a space for mutual growth and understanding.

1. Encourage Storytelling in Others

Inspire others to share their own myths by creating a safe and supportive environment.

Tips for Encouraging Storytelling:

- Share your story first to model vulnerability and authenticity.
- Ask open-ended questions to invite others to reflect on their journeys.
- Celebrate and validate the stories that others share.

Example:

Host a storytelling circle where participants share their experiences and connect over common themes.

2. Create Shared Experiences

Collaborative activities, such as workshops or group projects, allow you to build relationships through shared exploration of myths.

Ideas for Shared Experiences:

- Co-create art, music, or writing inspired by common themes.
- Organize a group ritual or ceremony to honor shared transitions or milestones.
- Lead discussions or journaling sessions focused on exploring personal narratives.

3. Foster a Sense of Belonging

Use your myth to create a sense of community and belonging, offering others a space where they feel seen, valued, and connected.

Ways to Foster Belonging:

- Acknowledge and celebrate the diverse experiences of your audience.
- Use inclusive language and symbols that resonate with a wide range of people.
- Share stories that highlight the universality of human experiences.

Example:

If your myth focuses on overcoming isolation, create a group or online forum where participants can connect and support one another.

The Ripple Effect of Inspiring Others

When you use your myth as a tool for connection, its impact extends far beyond your immediate audience. Each person you inspire carries forward the lessons, symbols, and insights of your story, creating a ripple effect of growth and transformation.

The Ripple Effect in Action:

1. **Empowered Individuals**: Your story inspires others to take action and embrace their own growth.
2. **Connected Communities**: Shared stories foster deeper relationships and mutual understanding.
3. **Collective Growth**: As more people share their myths, the collective narrative evolves, reflecting shared values and aspirations.

Moving Forward: Living as a Mythic Connector

Using your myth as a tool for connection is an ongoing journey. As you continue to share, listen, and collaborate, you will discover new ways to inspire and uplift those around you.

Key Takeaways:

- Myths are universal, offering symbols and lessons that resonate with diverse audiences.
- Inspiring others requires authenticity, vulnerability, and a focus on relatable themes.
- Building relationships through shared myths fosters understanding, community, and growth.

Reflection Questions:

- How can I use my myth to inspire and connect with others?
- What opportunities exist to share my story in a meaningful way?
- How can I encourage and support others in sharing their own myths?

Chapter 23: Myths in the Modern World: Adapting to the Digital Age

The digital age has revolutionized how we share, shape, and interact with stories. In a world interconnected by technology, personal myths are no longer confined to private reflections or intimate storytelling circles. They now have the potential to reach global audiences, transcend cultural boundaries, and inspire on an unprecedented scale. However, this new landscape also comes with challenges: authenticity, attention spans, and the influence of algorithmic curation can complicate how myths are told and received.

This chapter explores the role of myths in the modern digital world, offering strategies for adapting your personal narrative to thrive in a technology-driven age. From social media to virtual communities, we'll delve into how myths can be shared, expanded, and celebrated in ways that connect deeply with contemporary audiences.

The Evolution of Myths in the Digital Age

Historically, myths were passed down orally, inscribed on stone, or written in sacred texts. Today, the mediums have shifted dramatically, but the core function of myths—connecting, inspiring, and guiding—remains unchanged.

Key Changes in Mythmaking:

1. **Global Accessibility**: Digital platforms make it possible to share myths with audiences across the globe, fostering cross-cultural connections.
2. **Visual and Interactive Formats**: From memes to short videos, storytelling has become more visual and interactive, engaging audiences in dynamic ways.
3. **Speed of Dissemination**: Stories can go viral in hours, amplifying their impact but also increasing the pressure to captivate quickly.
4. **Decentralized Storytelling**: Anyone can share their story, democratizing mythmaking but also creating a crowded narrative landscape.

The Role of Personal Myths Online

Personal myths have found a new stage in the digital realm, where they can inspire, educate, and foster connection. Sharing your myth online allows you to reach diverse audiences and participate in a broader collective narrative.

Benefits of Sharing Myths Digitally:

- **Expanded Reach**: Platforms like Instagram, TikTok, and YouTube enable you to share your story with a vast audience.
- **Community Building**: Online communities allow you to connect with others who resonate with your journey.
- **Creative Expression**: Digital tools offer new ways to express your myth through visuals, music, and interactive media.
- **Legacy**: Digital storytelling preserves your narrative for future generations.

Challenges of Mythmaking in the Digital Age

While the digital world offers incredible opportunities, it also presents unique challenges. Understanding and navigating these challenges ensures that your myth remains authentic and impactful.

Common Challenges:

1. **Authenticity vs. Curation**: The pressure to present a polished version of your story can conflict with the authenticity of your myth.
2. **Oversaturation**: In a sea of content, it can be difficult to ensure your myth stands out and reaches the right audience.
3. **Short Attention Spans**: Audiences often favor short, engaging content, which may limit the depth of your storytelling.
4. **Algorithmic Influence**: Platform algorithms can shape how and when your story is seen, affecting its reach and reception.

Reflection Questions:

- How can I balance authenticity with the curated nature of digital storytelling?
- What strategies can I use to make my myth stand out in a crowded landscape?

Strategies for Adapting Myths to the Digital Age

To thrive in the digital age, storytellers must embrace the tools, platforms, and trends that define modern communication while staying true to their narrative.

1. Choose the Right Platforms

Each digital platform has unique strengths and audiences. Selecting the right ones ensures your myth resonates with those who need to hear it.

Platform Characteristics:

- **Instagram**: Ideal for visual storytelling and building an engaged community through posts, reels, and stories.
- **TikTok**: Perfect for short, creative videos that highlight key themes or moments of your myth.
- **YouTube**: Best for in-depth storytelling, tutorials, or personal narratives in video format.
- **Twitter**: Effective for sharing bite-sized insights, reflections, and connecting with like-minded individuals.
- **Blogs/Medium**: Suitable for long-form storytelling and deeper exploration of your myth.

Exercise:

Identify the platforms where your audience is most active and experiment with different formats to find what resonates.

2. Craft Content for Short Attention Spans

In the digital age, content needs to capture attention quickly while conveying meaningful ideas.

Tips for Engaging Content:

- Use **hooks** in the first few seconds of a video or opening lines of a post.
- Focus on **key moments or symbols** from your myth to create intrigue.
- Incorporate **visuals and music** to enhance emotional impact.
- Break down complex themes into **digestible pieces** that invite curiosity.

Example:

Instead of sharing your entire myth at once, post a short reel focusing on a transformative moment, such as "The day I found my courage."

3. Leverage Visual Storytelling

Visual elements make your myth more accessible and emotionally resonant. Digital tools offer endless possibilities for creative expression.

Ideas for Visual Storytelling:

- Create infographics or illustrations of key symbols and motifs from your myth.
- Share behind-the-scenes photos or videos that showcase your journey.
- Use color, lighting, and composition to evoke the mood of your narrative.
- Design storyboards or animations that bring your myth to life.

Exercise:

Choose a pivotal scene or symbol from your myth and represent it visually through photography, drawing, or digital design.

4. Foster Interaction and Engagement

Interactive storytelling invites your audience to participate in your myth, deepening their connection to your narrative.

Ways to Foster Interaction:

- Ask reflective questions or invite comments on your posts.
- Host live Q&A sessions or storytelling workshops online.
- Create polls or challenges related to themes in your myth.
- Share user-generated content that resonates with your narrative.

Example:

If your myth involves overcoming self-doubt, invite your audience to share their own stories of resilience using a specific hashtag.

5. Balance Depth and Accessibility

While short content is effective, it's also important to offer deeper insights for those who want to engage more fully with your story.

Tips for Balancing Depth:

- Use short content as a gateway to longer formats (e.g., link a TikTok video to a blog post).
- Offer layered storytelling, where each piece builds on the previous one.
- Share behind-the-scenes or extended versions of your story for those seeking more detail.

Exercise:

Create a content ladder where shorter, more accessible pieces lead to longer, in-depth explorations of your myth.

6. Stay Authentic Amid Trends

Trends can enhance visibility but should align with your story and values. Avoid compromising your authenticity for temporary popularity.

Tips for Authenticity:

- Adapt trends to fit your narrative rather than forcing your story to fit a trend.
- Focus on the core message of your myth and let that guide your content.
- Be consistent in your tone, style, and values across platforms.

Reflection:

What aspects of your myth are non-negotiable, even in a trend-driven environment?

Building a Digital Community Around Your Myth

The digital age enables you to build communities centered on shared experiences and values. By creating spaces where people can connect through your myth, you amplify its impact.

Steps to Build a Community:

1. **Identify Shared Themes**: Focus on universal aspects of your myth, such as transformation or resilience.
2. **Create Interactive Spaces**: Use forums, groups, or social media communities to encourage dialogue.
3. **Offer Value**: Share insights, resources, or tools that help others navigate their own myths.
4. **Celebrate Contributions**: Highlight and amplify the stories and input of your community members.

Example:

Create a private Facebook group or Discord server for people to share their own myths, connect, and learn from one another.

Embracing the Future of Mythmaking

As technology evolves, so will the ways we share and interact with myths. Virtual reality, augmented reality, and AI offer exciting possibilities for immersive storytelling, allowing your myth to take on new dimensions.

Emerging Trends:

- **Virtual Reality (VR)**: Create immersive experiences where audiences can explore your mythic world.
- **Augmented Reality (AR)**: Use AR to bring symbols or characters from your myth into real-world spaces.
- **AI Storytelling**: Leverage AI tools to co-create or enhance your narrative.

Reflection:

How can you incorporate emerging technologies to enrich your myth and engage your audience?

Moving Forward: Sharing Myths in a Digital World

The digital age offers unparalleled opportunities for storytelling, but it requires thoughtful adaptation to ensure your myth remains authentic and impactful. By embracing modern tools and platforms, you can share your journey in ways that resonate deeply, inspire others, and create lasting connections.

Key Takeaways:

- Myths thrive in the digital age when they are accessible, authentic, and visually engaging.
- The right platforms and formats amplify your story's reach and impact.
- Building a digital community around your myth fosters connection and collective growth.

Reflection Questions:

- How can I adapt my myth to resonate in a digital format?
- What platforms and tools best align with my storytelling style?
- How can I use my myth to inspire and connect with a global audience?

Chapter 24: Collective Shadowplay: Building a Community of Myths

While individual myths reflect personal journeys, the collective myth emerges from shared experiences, values, and aspirations. By weaving together individual narratives into a communal fabric, we can create a powerful, unified story that fosters connection, mutual growth, and collective transformation. This process—collective shadowplay—involves acknowledging shared challenges, illuminating collective shadows, and celebrating the diverse threads of individual myths.

This chapter explores the significance of collective shadowplay and provides strategies for building and sustaining a community of myths. You will learn how to create spaces for shared storytelling, address the challenges of communal shadow work, and cultivate an environment where personal and collective growth thrive in harmony.

The Importance of Collective Myths

Myths have always been a cornerstone of community. From ancient epics to modern movements, collective myths provide a sense of belonging, purpose, and shared identity. In the digital age, these myths transcend physical borders, creating global communities united by shared values and aspirations.

Key Functions of Collective Myths:

1. **Fostering Belonging**: Collective myths create a sense of unity and shared identity.
2. **Addressing Shared Challenges**: They provide a framework for understanding and addressing societal or communal issues.
3. **Inspiring Action**: By highlighting shared goals, collective myths motivate individuals to contribute to a larger purpose.
4. **Illuminating Collective Shadows**: They help communities confront and integrate shared fears, biases, or limitations.

Reflection:

What collective myths resonate with your community or audience? How does your personal myth contribute to these larger narratives?

What Is Collective Shadowplay?

Collective shadowplay involves the recognition and exploration of the shared "shadow" within a community. These are the unspoken fears, conflicts, and biases that shape group dynamics but are often overlooked. By engaging in collective shadowplay, communities can address these challenges, transform them into opportunities for growth, and create a more authentic and inclusive collective story.

Key Elements of Collective Shadowplay:

1. **Acknowledgment**: Recognizing the existence of collective shadows, such as prejudice, fear, or resistance to change.
2. **Dialogue**: Creating safe spaces for open discussion and exploration of these shared challenges.
3. **Integration**: Transforming collective shadows into strengths through empathy, understanding, and action.
4. **Celebration**: Honoring the diversity and resilience of the community as part of its collective myth.

Building a Community of Myths

Creating a community of myths requires intention, collaboration, and a commitment to fostering connection and growth. The following steps provide a framework for bringing individuals together to share, explore, and weave their narratives into a collective story.

Step 1: Establish a Shared Purpose

Every community of myths begins with a shared purpose or vision that unites its members. This purpose serves as the foundation for the collective myth.

Questions to Define Purpose:

- What values, goals, or challenges unite the members of this community?
- What themes or symbols resonate with the group's shared experiences?
- How can the collective myth empower and inspire its members?

Example:

A community focused on resilience might create a collective myth centered around the phoenix, symbolizing shared growth and renewal after hardship.

Step 2: Create Safe Spaces for Storytelling

Safe spaces encourage individuals to share their personal myths, fostering vulnerability, trust, and connection.

Tips for Creating Safe Spaces:

- **Inclusivity**: Ensure all voices are welcomed and valued, regardless of background or perspective.
- **Confidentiality**: Respect privacy and create boundaries that protect members' trust.
- **Empathy**: Approach every story with compassion and an open mind.
- **Facilitation**: Use prompts, rituals, or activities to guide and structure storytelling sessions.

Exercise:

Host a storytelling circle where members share pivotal moments from their personal myths. Use reflective prompts such as, "What challenge has shaped you the most?" or "What symbol represents your journey?"

Step 3: Illuminate the Collective Shadow

Engaging with the collective shadow involves identifying and addressing shared fears, biases, or conflicts within the community.

Steps for Collective Shadow Work:

1. **Identify the Shadow**: Reflect on recurring tensions, unspoken fears, or patterns of resistance within the group.
2. **Open Dialogue**: Facilitate discussions that explore the origins and impact of these shadows.
3. **Practice Empathy**: Encourage members to listen without judgment and seek understanding.
4. **Develop Solutions**: Collaborate on actions or rituals that transform the shadow into a source of strength.

Example:

If a community struggles with fear of failure, create a group ritual where members write down their fears, burn them symbolically, and share affirmations of resilience.

Step 4: Weave Individual Myths into the Collective Story

A community of myths thrives when individual stories are celebrated as integral parts of the collective narrative.

Ways to Weave Individual Myths:

- Highlight individual contributions or experiences in group discussions or events.
- Use symbols, rituals, or themes that reflect the diversity of members' stories.
- Create collaborative projects, such as a group art piece or anthology, that integrates multiple myths.

Example:

A group might create a collective mural where each member contributes a symbol representing their personal myth, forming a shared tapestry of stories.

Step 5: Foster Connection and Collaboration
Communities of myths are sustained through meaningful relationships and collaborative efforts. Encourage members to support and inspire one another.
Ideas for Fostering Connection:

- Pair members as "myth partners" to share and reflect on their narratives.
- Organize group activities, such as workshops or retreats, focused on collective storytelling.
- Use digital platforms to maintain connection and share updates between in-person gatherings.

Exercise:
Host a collaborative storytelling session where members build a shared narrative, each adding a chapter or perspective to the story.

Step 6: Celebrate the Collective Myth
Celebration honors the growth, resilience, and creativity of the community, reinforcing its shared identity and values.
Ways to Celebrate:

- Host an event or ritual to mark milestones in the group's journey.
- Create a shared artifact, such as a book, video, or art installation, that represents the collective myth.
- Share the group's story with a broader audience, inspiring others with its message.

Example:
A community might publish a digital zine featuring stories, poems, and artwork from its members, symbolizing their collective myth.

Overcoming Challenges in Building a Community of Myths

Building a community of myths is rewarding but can also present challenges. Addressing these with intention ensures the group remains cohesive and supportive.

Common Challenges:

1. **Conflict**: Differences in perspectives or priorities may create tension.
   ◦ **Solution**: Facilitate open dialogue and focus on shared values.
2. **Engagement**: Maintaining consistent participation can be difficult.
   ◦ **Solution**: Regularly update activities, offer diverse ways to participate, and celebrate contributions.
3. **Resistance to Shadow Work**: Some members may be hesitant to explore collective shadows.
   ◦ **Solution**: Approach shadow work gently, emphasizing its role in growth and transformation.

The Impact of Collective Shadowplay

Engaging in collective shadowplay and building a community of myths creates profound ripple effects, both within the group and in the larger world.

Benefits of Collective Shadowplay:

- **Stronger Connections**: Shared storytelling fosters trust, empathy, and a sense of belonging.
- **Collective Growth**: Addressing shared challenges enhances the group's resilience and cohesion.
- **Inspiration for Others**: The community's myth serves as a model for other groups, spreading its message and values.

Moving Forward: Sustaining a Community of Myths

A thriving community of myths requires ongoing attention, adaptation, and celebration. By prioritizing connection, inclusion, and creativity, you can sustain a group that inspires and supports its members while contributing to the broader collective narrative.

Key Takeaways:

- Collective myths unify individuals through shared purpose, values, and growth.
- Safe spaces, collaboration, and celebration are essential for building a strong community.
- Addressing collective shadows transforms challenges into opportunities for connection and empowerment.

Reflection Questions:

- How can I contribute my personal myth to a collective story?
- What steps can I take to foster a community of myths in my own life?
- How can this community's collective myth inspire and uplift others?

Chapter 25: Leaving a Legacy: Your Myth as a Gift for Future Generations

The culmination of a mythic journey is not its conclusion, but its transformation into a legacy—a gift that transcends time and space, touching the lives of others long after your story has been written. Leaving a legacy ensures that your myth, with all its lessons, triumphs, and challenges, continues to inspire, guide, and empower future generations. It is the ultimate act of storytelling, where your narrative becomes a thread in the fabric of collective human experience.

In this chapter, we explore how to preserve, share, and celebrate your myth as a legacy. From documenting your journey to fostering traditions and creating enduring works of art, you will learn to transform your personal story into a timeless source of wisdom and connection.

The Meaning of a Legacy

A legacy is the enduring impact of your life's journey. It is not limited to material wealth or achievements; it encompasses the values, insights, and inspiration you leave behind. A legacy rooted in your personal myth is a living gift, one that continues to grow and evolve through the people it touches.

Key Elements of a Legacy:

1. **Preservation**: Ensuring your story is accessible to future generations.
2. **Impact**: Creating meaning and value for those who encounter your myth.
3. **Continuity**: Connecting your narrative to the broader human story.
4. **Authenticity**: Staying true to the essence of your journey and values.

Reflection:

What do you want your myth to contribute to the world? How do you hope it will influence future generations?

Why Leave a Legacy?

Leaving a legacy allows your myth to extend its influence, creating ripples of inspiration that outlive you. It ensures that the lessons of your journey remain alive, offering guidance and hope to others.

Benefits of Leaving a Legacy:

1. **Inspiration**: Your myth becomes a beacon for those navigating similar challenges.
2. **Connection**: Sharing your story fosters a sense of continuity and belonging across generations.
3. **Empowerment**: Your narrative empowers others to embrace their own journeys.
4. **Immortality**: Through your legacy, your myth becomes part of a timeless, collective narrative.

Example:

The works of mythic storytellers like Joseph Campbell continue to shape and inspire long after their lifetimes, connecting countless people to universal truths.

How to Leave a Legacy Through Your Myth

Creating a legacy involves intentional action, reflection, and creativity. The following steps will guide you in transforming your myth into an enduring gift.

Step 1: Preserve Your Story

The first step in leaving a legacy is to ensure that your myth is documented and accessible. This involves recording your narrative in formats that can be shared and revisited.

Ways to Preserve Your Myth:

- **Writing**: Create a memoir, journal, or blog detailing your journey.
- **Audio/Visual**: Record podcasts, videos, or voice memos that capture your story in your own words.
- **Art**: Use paintings, sculptures, or digital media to represent key symbols and themes from your myth.
- **Archives**: Compile your works into a digital or physical archive, such as a family library or online repository.

Exercise:

Choose a medium that resonates with you and start documenting the key chapters of your myth. Focus on pivotal moments, lessons, and symbols.

Step 2: Share Your Story

Preservation is only the beginning. To leave a lasting legacy, your myth must be shared with others in ways that resonate and inspire.

Ways to Share Your Myth:

- **Publish**: Share your story through books, articles, or online platforms.
- **Teach**: Lead workshops, courses, or mentorship programs that integrate your narrative.
- **Perform**: Use storytelling, theater, or music to bring your myth to life for an audience.
- **Social Media**: Use platforms like Instagram, TikTok, or YouTube to share your myth in digestible, engaging formats.

Example:

A person whose myth centers on resilience might create a TED Talk or a social media series highlighting key lessons from their journey.

Step 3: Foster Traditions and Practices

Traditions are one of the most enduring ways to pass down your myth. By embedding your story into rituals, celebrations, or practices, you ensure that its essence remains alive in the lives of others.

Examples of Traditions:

- **Family Rituals**: Create annual or seasonal rituals that honor the themes of your myth.
- **Community Events**: Organize gatherings or ceremonies that celebrate shared values inspired by your story.
- **Personal Practices**: Teach meditation, journaling, or creative exercises that reflect your journey.

Exercise:

Design a ritual or practice based on a key lesson or symbol from your myth. Share it with family, friends, or your community.

Step 4: Create Enduring Works

Timeless works—whether artistic, literary, or symbolic—carry your myth into the future. These creations serve as touchstones for those who encounter them, inviting reflection and connection.

Examples of Enduring Works:

- **Books**: Write a novel, poetry collection, or nonfiction book based on your myth.
- **Art Installations**: Create a sculpture or mural that encapsulates the essence of your story.
- **Symbolic Artifacts**: Design jewelry, tokens, or tools that carry the energy of your myth.

Example:

An artist might create a series of paintings inspired by their mythic journey and donate them to a public gallery, where they inspire countless visitors.

Step 5: Inspire Future Storytellers

A true legacy encourages others to tell their own stories. By mentoring, teaching, or collaborating with emerging storytellers, you amplify the impact of your myth.

Ways to Inspire Storytellers:

- Offer guidance and support to those beginning their storytelling journeys.
- Collaborate on creative projects that integrate multiple myths.
- Create resources, such as guides or toolkits, to help others craft their narratives.

Example:

An experienced storyteller might host workshops for young writers, helping them explore and express their personal myths.

Step 6: Reflect on Your Impact

Leaving a legacy is an ongoing process. Reflecting on the impact of your myth allows you to adapt and refine how it is shared.

Questions for Reflection:

- How has my story influenced others so far?
- What new ways can I share or celebrate my myth?
- What feedback or responses have I received, and how can they guide my next steps?

Exercise:

Create a "Legacy Journal" where you record the ways your myth has impacted others and ideas for expanding its reach.

Overcoming Challenges in Legacy Building

Leaving a legacy can feel overwhelming, but with focus and intention, these challenges can become opportunities for growth.

Common Challenges:

1. **Self-Doubt**: Questioning whether your story is worthy of a legacy.
   - **Solution**: Reflect on how your story has already inspired others and trust in its value.
2. **Longevity**: Ensuring your myth endures over time.
   - **Solution**: Use multiple formats and platforms to preserve your story.
3. **Relevance**: Adapting your myth to resonate with future audiences.
   - **Solution**: Focus on universal themes and values that transcend time.

The Ripple Effect of Your Legacy

Your myth, as a legacy, creates a ripple effect that extends far beyond your immediate circle. It becomes a source of inspiration, guidance, and connection for people you may never meet.

Examples of Ripple Effects:

- A memoir inspires a reader to embrace resilience and overcome adversity.
- A family tradition rooted in your myth brings generations closer together.
- A workshop you lead sparks the creation of new myths by participants.

Moving Forward: Embracing Your Myth's Legacy

As you prepare to leave a legacy, remember that it is not about perfection but intention. Your myth is a living story, and its impact will continue to evolve and expand through the lives it touches.

Key Takeaways:

- A legacy is the lasting impact of your myth, offering inspiration and guidance to future generations.
- Preservation, sharing, and fostering traditions ensure your story endures.
- Inspiring others to tell their own myths amplifies the reach and impact of your legacy.

Reflection Questions:

- What is the most important message or lesson of my myth?
- How can I ensure my story inspires and empowers future generations?
- What steps can I take today to begin creating my legacy?

With this final chapter, you have reached the culmination of your mythic journey. But remember, every ending is also a new beginning. As you leave your legacy, you create space for new myths to emerge—yours and others'—ensuring the story continues to unfold in infinite, meaningful ways.

Appendix A: Exercises for Shadow Exploration and Integration

Exploring and integrating your shadow—the hidden parts of yourself that you suppress or deny—is an essential part of personal growth and transformation. Shadow work allows you to confront fears, embrace vulnerabilities, and uncover untapped strengths. This appendix provides practical exercises to help you engage with your shadow, fostering self-awareness, healing, and empowerment.

Section 1: Understanding the Shadow

Before diving into the exercises, it's important to understand the concept of the shadow. Coined by Carl Jung, the shadow represents the unconscious aspects of ourselves, including fears, insecurities, and desires that we may hide from ourselves and others. Shadow work involves bringing these aspects into conscious awareness, allowing us to accept and integrate them.

Section 2: Exercises for Shadow Exploration

The following exercises are designed to help you uncover and explore your shadow. Approach them with curiosity, compassion, and a willingness to engage deeply with yourself.

Exercise 1: Identifying the Shadow Through Emotional Triggers

Our shadow often reveals itself through emotional triggers—moments when we overreact or feel intense emotions in response to a situation or person.

Steps:

1. **Recall a Recent Trigger**: Think of a recent situation where you felt angry, jealous, defensive, or overly critical.
2. **Describe the Trigger**: Write down what happened and how it made you feel. Be as detailed as possible.
3. **Ask Reflective Questions**:
   - Why did this situation affect me so strongly?
   - What fear or insecurity might this reaction reveal?
   - Is there a part of myself that I see reflected in the trigger?
4. **Acknowledge the Shadow**: Write down any insights you uncover, framing them with compassion. For example, "I feel jealous because I fear I'm not good enough. This is a part of myself I want to understand and heal."

Exercise 2: Dialogue with Your Shadow

Engaging in a dialogue with your shadow can help you understand its motivations, fears, and desires.

Steps:

1. **Create a Safe Space**: Find a quiet place where you can reflect without interruptions.
2. **Visualize Your Shadow**: Close your eyes and imagine your shadow as a person, animal, or abstract form.
3. **Write a Conversation**: In a journal, write a dialogue between yourself and your shadow. Use prompts like:
    - "What are you afraid of?"
    - "What do you want me to know about you?"
    - "How can we work together to grow?"
4. **Reflect**: Review the conversation and note any insights or patterns.

Exercise 3: Exploring Shadow Through Projection

Projection occurs when we attribute our shadow traits to others. Exploring these projections can reveal hidden aspects of ourselves.

Steps:

1. **Identify a Projection**: Think of someone you strongly dislike or criticize. Write down the traits or behaviors that bother you most about them.
2. **Turn the Mirror Inward**: Ask yourself:
    - Do I possess these traits, even in subtle ways?
    - Have I suppressed or denied this part of myself?
3. **Reflect and Reframe**: Write about how you can accept or channel these traits in a healthy way. For example, if you resent someone's assertiveness, explore how you can cultivate assertiveness in your own life.

Exercise 4: Shadow Mapping

Shadow mapping is a visual exercise that helps you identify and organize the elements of your shadow.

Steps:

1. **Draw a Circle**: On a piece of paper, draw a large circle and label it "My Shadow."
2. **Divide into Sections**: Divide the circle into sections for different aspects of your shadow, such as fears, insecurities, hidden desires, or unexpressed emotions.
3. **Fill in the Sections**: Write down words, phrases, or images that represent each section.
4. **Reflect**: Spend time considering how these elements influence your thoughts, behaviors, and relationships.

Section 3: Exercises for Shadow Integration

Integration involves accepting and working with your shadow, transforming it into a source of strength and wholeness.

Exercise 5: Shadow Affirmation Practice

This exercise helps you reframe and accept shadow traits with compassion and understanding.

Steps:

1. **Identify a Shadow Trait**: Choose a trait you've uncovered, such as jealousy, fear, or anger.
2. **Reframe the Trait**: Reflect on how this trait might serve you positively. For example:
    ◦ Anger can indicate a boundary that needs to be set.
    ◦ Jealousy can highlight something you aspire to achieve.
3. **Write an Affirmation**: Create a compassionate statement, such as:
    ◦ "I acknowledge my anger as a signal to protect my well-being."
    ◦ "My jealousy shows me what I truly value."
4. **Repeat Daily**: Say the affirmation aloud or write it in a journal each day.

Exercise 6: Shadow Embodiment

This somatic exercise allows you to physically express and release shadow aspects.

Steps:

1. **Choose a Shadow Emotion**: Identify an emotion you want to explore, such as fear, sadness, or frustration.
2. **Set the Scene**: Find a private space and play music that resonates with the emotion.
3. **Move Freely**: Use your body to express the emotion. For example:
    ◦ Stomp your feet to embody frustration.
    ◦ Curl into a ball to express sadness.
4. **Reflect and Release**: Afterward, journal about how the exercise felt and any insights you gained.

Exercise 7: Shadow Integration Ritual

Rituals provide a structured way to honor and integrate your shadow into your life.

Steps:

1. **Choose a Symbol**: Select an object or image that represents your shadow, such as a stone, feather, or drawing.
2. **Create a Sacred Space**: Arrange candles, incense, or meaningful items to set the mood.
3. **Write an Intention**: Write a statement acknowledging your shadow and your intention to work with it. For example:
    ◦ "I honor my fear as a part of myself and invite it to teach me courage."
4. **Perform the Ritual**: Hold the symbol, read your intention aloud, and meditate on your shadow.

5. **Keep the Symbol**: Place the symbol somewhere meaningful as a reminder of your commitment to integration.

Exercise 8: Shadow Storytelling

Turning your shadow into a narrative helps you make sense of its role in your life.

Steps:

1. **Personify the Shadow**: Write a story where your shadow is a character, such as a mentor, guide, or rival.
2. **Describe Its Journey**: Explore how this character interacts with you and influences your life.
3. **Write a Resolution**: Conclude the story with a moment of understanding, collaboration, or transformation.
4. **Reflect**: Consider how this story mirrors your real-life experiences and growth.

Section 4: Closing Reflection

Shadow exploration and integration are ongoing processes that deepen over time. As you engage with these exercises, remember to approach your shadow with compassion, patience, and curiosity. Each step brings you closer to wholeness, unlocking the hidden gifts and wisdom within.

Final Reflection Questions:

- What have I learned about myself through these exercises?
- How has my relationship with my shadow evolved?
- What steps can I take to continue integrating my shadow into my life?

By exploring and integrating your shadow, you embrace the fullness of your humanity, transforming hidden fears into powerful allies on your mythic journey.

Appendix B: Recommended Resources on Mythology, Psychology, and Personal Growth

This appendix provides a curated list of books, articles, podcasts, films, and online resources to deepen your understanding of mythology, psychology, and personal growth. These resources will help you explore the themes discussed in this book, inspire further self-discovery, and provide practical tools for continuing your mythic journey.

Section 1: Mythology

Mythology serves as the foundation for understanding universal narratives, archetypes, and symbols. These resources explore myths from various cultures and their relevance to modern life.

Books on Mythology

1. **The Hero with a Thousand Faces** by Joseph Campbell
   - Explores the archetypal hero's journey and its presence across global myths.
2. **Mythos** by Stephen Fry
   - A retelling of Greek myths in an engaging and accessible style.
3. **The Power of Myth** by Joseph Campbell and Bill Moyers
   - A conversational exploration of myths and their enduring relevance to humanity.
4. **Women Who Run with the Wolves** by Clarissa Pinkola Estés
   - Examines myths and fairy tales through the lens of the Wild Woman archetype.
5. **The Masks of God (4-Volume Series)** by Joseph Campbell
   - A comprehensive exploration of mythology across different cultures and traditions.

Articles and Essays

- "Why Mythology Is Still Relevant in the Modern World" by Karen Armstrong (*The Guardian*)
- "The Enduring Appeal of Mythic Stories" by Jean Shinoda Bolen (*Psychology Today*)

Podcasts

1. **Mythology** by Parcast Network
   - Retellings of myths from around the world with historical and cultural insights.
2. **The History of Philosophy Without Any Gaps** (Episodes on Myths in Ancient Philosophy)
   - Explores how ancient philosophers integrated mythology into their teachings.

Films and Documentaries

1. **Joseph Campbell and the Power of Myth** (PBS Series)
   ◦ A six-part series exploring mythic themes in human history.
2. **Mythic Journeys** (2009)
   ◦ A documentary exploring the relevance of myths in contemporary society.
3. **Black Orpheus** (1959)
   ◦ A retelling of the Orpheus myth set in Rio de Janeiro during Carnival.

Section 2: Psychology

Understanding the psychological underpinnings of myths and personal growth can deepen your shadow work and self-discovery. These resources provide foundational insights into Jungian psychology, shadow integration, and emotional healing.

Books on Psychology

1. **Man and His Symbols** by Carl G. Jung
   ◦ A comprehensive introduction to Jung's theories of archetypes and the unconscious.
2. **The Archetypes and the Collective Unconscious** by Carl G. Jung
   ◦ An in-depth exploration of archetypes and their role in shaping human behavior.
3. **Owning Your Own Shadow** by Robert A. Johnson
   ◦ A practical guide to understanding and integrating the shadow.
4. **The Undiscovered Self** by Carl G. Jung
   ◦ Discusses the tension between individual psychology and societal forces.
5. **Embracing Our Selves** by Hal Stone and Sidra Stone
   ◦ Explores voice dialogue as a tool for integrating different aspects of the self.

Articles and Essays

- "The Shadow: A Psychological Concept of Invaluable Insight" by David Tacey (*Journal of Analytical Psychology*)
- "Integrating the Shadow: The Path to Wholeness" by Christine Caldwell (*Psych Central*)

Podcasts

1. **This Jungian Life**
   ◦ Hosts discuss Jungian psychology concepts and their application to modern life.
2. **Unlocking Us with Brené Brown**
   ◦ Explores topics such as vulnerability, courage, and emotional growth.
3. **The Hidden Brain**
   ◦ Focuses on the unconscious patterns that drive human behavior.

Online Courses and Resources

- **Jung Platform** (jungplatform.com)
  - Offers courses, workshops, and articles on Jungian psychology.
- **Psychology Today: Shadow Work**
  - A collection of articles and tools for engaging in shadow exploration.

Section 3: Personal Growth

Personal growth involves integrating the lessons of mythology and psychology into daily life. These resources provide practical tools, inspiring stories, and frameworks for self-improvement and transformation.

Books on Personal Growth

1. **The Gifts of Imperfection** by Brené Brown
   - A guide to embracing vulnerability and authenticity.
2. **Atomic Habits** by James Clear
   - Offers practical advice for creating and sustaining positive habits.
3. **The Four Agreements** by Don Miguel Ruiz
   - A Toltec-inspired guide to personal freedom and growth.
4. **Daring Greatly** by Brené Brown
   - Explores how courage and vulnerability can transform relationships and self-worth.
5. **The Untethered Soul** by Michael A. Singer
   - Examines the path to inner peace and self-realization.

Articles and Essays

- "The Role of Storytelling in Personal Development" by Christina Baldwin (*The New Yorker*)
- "10 Ways to Cultivate Self-Awareness" by Tasha Eurich (*Harvard Business Review*)

Podcasts

1. **The School of Greatness** by Lewis Howes
   - Features interviews with experts on mindset, success, and self-improvement.
2. **On Being with Krista Tippett**
   - Conversations exploring meaning, faith, and personal growth.
3. **The Tony Robbins Podcast**
   - Focuses on strategies for success, transformation, and fulfillment.

Workshops and Tools

- **The Hoffman Process** (hoffmaninstitute.org)
  - ◦ A program for emotional healing and self-awareness.
- **Insight Timer** (insighttimer.com)
  - ◦ An app offering guided meditations and mindfulness exercises.

Section 4: Cross-Disciplinary Resources

The following resources integrate mythology, psychology, and personal growth, offering unique perspectives on the interplay between these fields.

Books

1. **The Mythic Imagination** by Stephen Larsen
   - ◦ Explores the intersection of myth, psychology, and creativity.
2. **Care of the Soul** by Thomas Moore
   - ◦ Discusses the role of myths and archetypes in nurturing the soul.
3. **Integral Psychology** by Ken Wilber
   - ◦ Combines Eastern and Western approaches to psychology and spirituality.

Online Communities

- **Mythosophia** (mythosophia.com)
  - ◦ A forum for discussing myths, archetypes, and personal growth.
- **Reddit: Jungian Psychology and Shadow Work**
  - ◦ A community for exploring Jungian ideas and sharing personal experiences.

Final Reflection

These resources are tools to deepen your understanding and enhance your practice of mythic storytelling, shadow work, and personal growth. As you engage with them, remember that the most powerful insights come from applying what you learn to your own journey.

Reflection Questions:

- Which resources resonate most with your current needs and interests?
- How can you incorporate these insights into your personal mythology?
- What new perspectives or tools do you hope to gain from these resources?

Your mythic journey is ever-evolving, and these resources are companions to guide you as you continue to explore, grow, and transform.

<u>Message from the Author:</u>

I hope you enjoyed this book, I love astrology and knew there was not a book such as this out on the shelf. I love metaphysical items as well. Please check out my other books:

-Life of Government Benefits

-My life of Hell

-My life with Hydrocephalus

-Red Sky

-World Domination:Woman's rule

-World Domination:Woman's Rule 2: The War

-Life and Banishment of Apophis: book 1

-The Kidney Friendly Diet

-The Ultimate Hemp Cookbook

-Creating a Dispensary(legally)

-Cleanliness throughout life: the importance of showering from childhood to adulthood.

-Strong Roots: The Risks of Overcoddling children

-Hemp Horoscopes: Cosmic Insights and Earthly Healing

- Celestial Hemp Navigating the Zodiac: Through the Green Cosmos

-Astrological Hemp: Aligning The Stars with Earth's Ancient Herb

-The Astrological Guide to Hemp: Stars, Signs, and Sacred Leaves

-Green Growth: Innovative Marketing Strategies for your Hemp Products and Dispensary

-Cosmic Cannabis

-Astrological Munchies

-Henry The Hemp

-Zodiacal Roots: The Astrological Soul Of Hemp

- Green Constellations: Intersection of Hemp and Zodiac

-Hemp in The Houses: An astrological Adventure Through The Cannabis Galaxy

-Galactic Ganja Guide

Heavenly Hemp

Zodiac Leaves

Doctor Who Astrology

Cannastrology

Stellar Satvias and Cosmic Indicas

<u>Celestial Cannabis: A Zodiac Journey</u>

AstroHerbology: The Sky and The Soil: Volume 1

AstroHerbology:Celestial Cannabis:Volume 2

Cosmic Cannabis Cultivation

The Starry Guide to Herbal Harmony: Volume 1

The Starry Guide to Herbal Harmony: Cannabis Universe: Volume 2

Yugioh Astrology: Astrological Guide to Deck, Duels and more

Nightmare Mansion: Echoes of The Abyss

Nightmare Mansion 2: Legacy of Shadows

Nightmare Mansion 3: Shadows of the Forgotten
Nightmare Mansion 4: Echoes of the Damned
The Life and Banishment of Apophis: Book 2
Nightmare Mansion: Halls of Despair
Healing with Herb: Cannabis and Hydrocephalus
Planetary Pot: Aligning with Astrological Herbs: Volume 1
Fast Track to Freedom: 30 Days to Financial Independence Using AI, Assets, and Agile Hustles
Cosmic Hemp Pathways
How to Become Financially Free in 30 Days: 10,000 Paths to Prosperity
Zodiacal Herbage: Astrological Insights: Volume 1
Nightmare Mansion: Whispers in the Walls
The Daleks Invade Atlantis
Henry the hemp and Hydrocephalus

10X The Kidney Friendly Diet
Cannabis Universe: Adult coloring book
Hemp Astrology: The Healing Power of the Stars
Zodiacal Herbage: Astrological Insights: Cannabis Universe: Volume 2
Planetary Pot: Aligning with Astrological Herbs: Cannabis Universes: Volume 2
Doctor Who Meets the Replicators and SG-1: The Ultimate Battle for Survival
Nightmare Mansion: Curse of the Blood Moon
The Celestial Stoner: A Guide to the Zodiac
Cosmic Pleasures: Sex Toy Astrology for Every Sign
Hydrocephalus Astrology: Navigating the Stars and Healing Waters
Lapis and the Mischievous Chocolate Bar

Celestial Positions: Sexual Astrology for Every Sign
Apophis's Shadow Work Journal: : A Journey of Self-Discovery and Healing
Kinky Cosmos: Sexual Kink Astrology for Every Sign
Digital Cosmos: The Astrological Digimon Compendium
Stellar Seeds: The Cosmic Guide to Growing with Astrology
Apophis's Daily Gratitude Journal

Cat Astrology: Feline Mysteries of the Cosmos
The Cosmic Kama Sutra: An Astrological Guide to Sexual Positions
Unleash Your Potential: A Guided Journal Powered by AI Insights
Whispers of the Enchanted Grove

Cosmic Pleasures: An Astrological Guide to Sexual Kinks
369, 12 Manifestation Journal

Whisper of the nocturne journal(blank journal for writing or drawing)
The Boogey Book
Locked In Reflection: A Chastity Journey Through Locktober
Generating Wealth Quickly:
How to Generate $100,000 in 24 Hours
Star Magic: Harness the Power of the Universe
The Flatulence Chronicles: A Fart Journal for Self-Discovery
The Doctor and The Death Moth
Seize the Day: A Personal Seizure Tracking Journal
The Ultimate Boogeyman Safari: A Journey into the Boogie World and Beyond
Whispers of Samhain: 1,000 Spells of Love, Luck, and Lunar Magic: Samhain Spell Book
Apophis's guides:
Witch's Spellbook Crafting Guide for Halloween
<u>Frost & Flame: The Enchanted Yule Grimoire of 1000 Winter Spells</u>
<u>The Ultimate Boogey Goo Guide & Spooky Activities for Halloween Fun</u>
Harmony of the Scales: A Libra's Spellcraft for Balance and Beauty
The Enchanted Advent: 36 Days of Christmas Wonders

Nightmare Mansion: The Labyrinth of Screams
Harvest of Enchantment: 1,000 Spells of Gratitude, Love, and Fortune for Thanksgiving
The Boogey Chronicles: A Journal of Nightly Encounters and Shadowy Secrets
The 12 Days of Financial Freedom: A Step-by-Step Christmas Countdown to Transform Your
Finances
Sigil of the Eternal Spiral Blank Journal
A Christmas Feast: Timeless Recipes for Every Meal
Holiday Stress-Free Solutions: A Survival Guide to Thriving During the Festive Season
Yu-Gi-Oh! Holiday Gifting Mastery: The Ultimate Guide for Fans and Newcomers Alike
Holiday Harmony: A Hydrocephalus Survival Guide for the Festive Season
Celestial Craft: The Witch's Almanac for 2025 – A Cosmic Guide to Manifestations, Moons,
and Mystical Events
Doctor Who: The Toymaker's Winter Wonderland
Tulsa King Unveiled: A Thrilling Guide to Stallone's Mafia Masterpiece
Pendulum Craft: A Complete Guide to Crafting and Using Personalized Divination Tools
Nightmare Mansion: Santa's Eternal Eve
Starlight Noel: A Cosmic Journey through Christmas Mysteries
The Dark Architect: Unlocking the Blueprint of Existence
Surviving the Embrace: The Ultimate Guide to Encounters with The Hugging Molly
The Enchanted Codex: Secrets of the Craft for Witches, Wiccans, and Pagans
Harvest of Gratitude: A Complete Thanksgiving Guide
Yuletide Essentials: A Complete Guide to an Authentic and Magical Christmas
Celestial Smokes: A Cosmic Guide to Cigars and Astrology

Living in Balance: A Comprehensive Survival Guide to Thriving with Diabetes Insipidus
Cosmic Symbiosis: The Venom Zodiac Chronicles
The Cursed Paw of Ambition
Cosmic Symbiosis: The Astrological Venom Journal
Celestial Wonders Unfold: A Stargazer's Guide to the Cosmos (2024-2029)
The Ultimate Black Friday Prepper's Guide: Mastering Shopping Strategies and Savings
Cosmic Sales: The Astrological Guide to Black Friday Shopping
Legends of the Corn Mother and Other Harvest Myths
Whispers of the Harvest: The Corn Mother's Journal
The Evergreen Spellbook
The Doctor Meets the Boogeyman
The White Witch of Rose Hall's SpellBook
The Gingerbread Golem's Shadow: A Study in Sweet Darkness
The Gingerbread Golem Codex: An Academic Exploration of Sweet Myths
The Gingerbread Golem Grimoire: Sweet Magicks and Spells for the Festive Witch
The Curse of the Gingerbread Golem
10-minute Christmas Crafts for kids
<u>Christmas Crisis Solutions: The Ultimate Last-Minute Survival Guide</u>
Gingerbread Golem Recipes: Holiday Treats with a Magical Twist
The Infinite Key: Unlocking Mystical Secrets of the Ages
Enchanted Yule: A Wiccan and Pagan Guide to a Magical and Memorable Season
Dinosaurs of Power: Unlocking Ancient Magick
Astro-Dinos: The Cosmic Guide to Prehistoric Wisdom
Gallifrey's Yule Logs: A Festive Doctor Who Cookbook
The Dino Grimoire: Secrets of Prehistoric Magick
The Gift They Never Knew They Needed
The Gingerbread Golem's Culinary Alchemy: Enchanting Recipes for a Sweetly Dark Feast
A Time Lord Christmas: Holiday Adventures with the Doctor
Krampusproofing Your Home: Defensive Strategies for Yule
Silent Frights: A Collection of Christmas Creepypastas to Chill Your Bones
Santa Raptor's Jolly Carnage: A Dino-Claus Christmas Tale
Prehistoric Palettes: A Dino Wicca Coloring Journey
The Christmas Wishkeeper Chronicles
The Starlight Sleigh: A Holiday Journey
Elf Secrets: The True Magic of the North Pole
Candy Cane Conjurations
Cooking with Kids: Recipes Under 20 Minutes
Doctor Who: The TARDIS Confiscation
The Anxiety First Aid Kit: Quick Tools to Calm Your Mind
Frosty Whispers: A Winter's Tale
The Infinite Key: Unlocking the Secrets to Prosperity, Resilience, and Purpose

The Grasping Void: Why You'll Regret This Purchase
Astrology for Busy Bees: Star Signs Simplified
The Instant Focus Formula: Cut Through the Noise
The Secret Language of Colors: Unlocking the Emotional Codes
Sacred Fossil Chronicles: Blank Journal
The Christmas Cottage Miracle
Feeding Frenzy: Graboid-Inspired Recipes
Manifest in Minutes: The Quick Law of Attraction Guide
The Symbiote Chronicles: Doctor Who's Venomous Journey
Think Tiny, Grow Big: The Minimalist Mindset
The Energy Key: Unlocking Limitless Motivation
New Year, New Magic: Manifesting Your Best Year Yet
Unstoppable You: Mastering Confidence in Minutes
Infinite Energy: The Secret to Never Feeling Drained
Lightning Focus: Mastering the Art of Productivity in a Distracted World
Saturnalia Manifestation Magick: A Guide to Unlocking Abundance During the Solstice
Graboids and Garland: The Ultimate Tremors-Themed Christmas Guide
12 Nights of Holiday Magic
The Power of Pause: 60-Second Mindfulness Practices
The Quick Reset: How to Reclaim Your Life After Burnout
The Shadow Eater: A Tale of Despair and Survival
The Micro-Mastery Method: Transform Your Skills in Just Minutes a Day
Reclaiming Time: How to Live More by Doing Less
Chronovore: The Eternal Nexus
The Mind Reset: Unlocking Your Inner Peace in a Chaotic World
Confidence Code: Building Unshakable Self-Belief
Baby the Vampire Terrier
Baby the Vampire Terrier's Christmas Adventure
Celestial Streams: The Content Creator's Astrology Manual
The Wealth Whisperer: Unlocking Abundance with Everyday Actions
The Energy Equation: Maximize Your Output Without Burning Out
The Happiness Algorithm: Science-Backed Steps to Joyful Living
Stress-Free Success: Achieving Goals Without Anxiety
Mindful Wealth: The New Blueprint for Financial Freedom
The Festive Flavors of New Year: A Culinary Celebration
The Master's Gambit: Keys of Eternal Power
Shadowed Secrets: Groundhog Day Mysteries
Beneath the Burrow: Lessons from the Groundhog
Spring's Whispers: The Groundhog's Prediction
The Limitless Mindset: Unlock Your Untapped Potential
The Focus Funnel: How to Cut Through Chaos and Get Results

Bold Moves: Building Courage to Live on Your Terms
The Daily Shift: Simple Practices for Lasting Transformation
The Quarter-Life Reset: Thriving in Your 20s and 30s
If you want solar for your home go here: https://www.harborsolar.live/apophisenterprises/

Bold Moves: Building Courage to Live on Your Terms
The Daily Shift: Simple Practices for Lasting Transformation
The Quarter-Life Reset: Thriving in Your 20s and 30s

Get Some Tarot cards: https://www.makeplayingcards.com/sell/apophis-occult-shop

Get some shirts: https://www.bonfire.com/store/apophis-shirt-emporium/

<u>Instagrams:</u>
@apophis_enterprises,
@apophisbookemporium,
@apophisscardshop
Twitter: @apophisenterpr1
Tiktok:@apophisenterprise
Youtube: @sg1fan23477, @FiresideRetreatKingdom
Hive: @sg1fan23477
CheeLee: @SG1fan23477
Podcast: Apophis Chat Zone: https://open.spotify.com/show/5zXbr-CLEV2xzCp8ybrfHsk?si=fb4d4fdbdce44dec

Newsletter: https://apophiss-newsletter-27c897.beehiiv.com/

If you want to support me or see posts of other projects that I have come over to: **buymeacof-fee.com/mpetchinskg**
I post there daily several times a day

Get your Dinowicca or Christmas themed digital products, especially Santa Raptor songs and other musics. Here: **https://sg1fan23477.gumroad.com**

Apophis Yuletide Digital has not only digital Christmas items, but it will have all things with Dinowicca as well as other Digital products.